Using Linux

(kernel version 2.0 to 2.2)

All trademarks quoted are the property of their respective editors.

All rights reserved. No part of this publication may be reproduced, stored in a retrieval system, or transmitted, in any form, or by any means, electronic, mechanical, photocopying, recording or otherwise, without the prior permission of the publishers.

Copyright - Editions ENI - Août 1999
ISBN: 2-7460-0534-4
Original edition: ISBN: 2-7460-0165-9

Editions ENI

BP 32125
44021 NANTES Cédex 1

Tel : 33.2.40.92.45.45
Fax : 33.2.40.92.45.46

e-mail : editions@ediENI.com

http:\\www.editions-eni.com

ENI Publishing LTD

500 Chiswick High Road
London W4 5RG

Tel: 0181 956 23 20
Fax: 0181 956 23 21

e-mail: publishing@ediENI.com

http:\\www.editions-eni.com

Autor: Bruno GUÉRIN
Collection directed by Joëlle MUSSET
Translated from the French by Andrew BLACKBURN

Table of contents

Chapter 1 — Overview

- **A.** What is Linux? **10**
- **B.** Purpose of this book **12**

Chapter 2 — Linux file system hierarchy

- **A.** The path concept **17**
- **B.** Presenting the Filesystem Hierarchy Standard .. **18**

Chapter 3 — Defining users and groups

- **A.** Users **24**
- **B.** Groups **26**

Chapter 4 — Logging in and entering your first commands

- **A.** Login procedure **30**
- **B.** General command presentation **32**
- **C.** Entering more than one command **34**

Using Linux

User owners and owner groups — Chapter 5

- **A.** Users and owner groups **44**
- **B.** Changing owner and group for a file **45**

Permission to access files and directories — Chapter 6

- **A.** Access permissions for files **48**
- **B.** Directory permissions **50**
- **C.** Modifying access permissions **51**
- **D.** Extended access permissions **54**

The Bash Shell — Chapter 7

- **A.** Overview **58**
- **B.** Entering commands **59**
- **C.** Editing a command **60**
- **D.** Aliases **63**
- **E.** History and command substitutions **66**

(kernel version 2.0 à 2.2)

F.	Environment variables	**74**
G.	Shell built-in commands	**76**
H.	Meta-characters and special characters	**89**
I.	Parsing the command line	**92**
J.	Initializing the environment	**93**
K.	Customizing the prompt	**95**

Redirecting inputs and outputs — Chapter 8

A.	Structure of a command	**98**
B.	Concept of standard streams	**100**
C.	Redirecting standard streams	**101**
D.	Connecting commands using pipes	**106**

The vi editor principal commands — Chapter 9

A.	Why vi ?	**108**
B.	Presenting vi	**108**

Using Linux

C.	Moving around in the text	**109**
D.	Correcting in command mode	**110**
E.	Replacing characters or character strings	**111**
F.	Searching for a character string	**112**
G.	Copying and moving text	**112**
H.	Command line mode: ex mode	**113**
I.	Configuring the editor	**114**

On-line help — Chapter 10

| A. | On-line help | **118** |
| B. | The man command | **119** |

Printing system — Chapter 11

| A. | Overview | **122** |
| B. | The BSD printing system | **123** |

(kernel version 2.0 à 2.2)

Regular expressions — Chapter 12

A.	Meta-characters	**128**
B.	Special characters	**129**

Handling files and directories — Chapter 13

A.	Creating directories	**134**
B.	Deleting directories	**136**
C.	Copying files and directories	**137**
D.	Moving files and directories	**139**
E.	Deleting files and directories	**140**
F.	Viewing files and directories	**141**
G.	File types	**145**
H.	Creating files and modifying timestamps	**145**
I.	Finding files and directories	**147**

Using Linux

Principal Linux commands — Chapter 14

- **A.** Processing file contents **152**
- **B.** Time Management **206**
- **C.** Message commands **218**
- **D.** Compressing files **226**
- **E.** Process management **236**

(kernel version 2.0 à 2.2)

Chapter 1

Overview

A. What is Linux ? **10**

B. Purpose of this book **12**

Linux is a Unix system that appeared in 1991. One of its main features is that it is totally free. Linux is not in the public domain however, as it is covered by the "copyleft" of the GNU project, which originated in the 1980's. At this time, in reaction to the commercialization of UNIX, Richard Stallman created the FSF (*free software foundation*) and made a lot of free software accessible to all. He called this software GNU, a recursive acronym short for *GNU is Not Unix*. To ensure that the source code remained freely accessible and would not be used for commercial purposes, a special license was created, called "copyleft". This copyleft allows complete freedom to anyone who wants to use, copy or modify the product under its protection, provided that the source code is always diffused freely and without hindrance.

Linux started as the hobby project of a student named Linus Torvalds who, using a lot of the GNU software, finally produced what has become the most popular freely available operating system in the world.

Strictly speaking, Linux is not in itself an operating system. It is a kernel, the *heart* of an operating system that forms the interface between the hardware, and the set of commands, utilities and system programs that are necessary to make up the operating system. These latter components are provided either by the FSF or by third parties and are generally diffused and protected by the same copyleft to prevent them from falling into commercial hands.

Neither can Linux really be called a Unix system, in the sense that the code of this kernel does not contain a single line of the code of the original AT&T Unix kernel. Initially, commercial Unix manufacturers had to buy this Unix code, but it has since been so extensively modified that, outside of any legal context, it is doubtful if this original code still contributes much to the product.

(kernel version 2.0 à 2.2)

To all intents and purposes however, Linux *is* a fully-fledged Unix system. It operates like a Unix system, and at least as well as one. It may sometimes lack certain graphical administration tools, although this deficiency has been partially remedied already in certain distributions. However, this criticism must be tempered by the fact that graphical tools generally rely on classical utilities, which are used by Linux. A good knowledge of these utilities promotes a better control of the system as, for all their conviviality, these graphical interfaces lack the full richness offered by line commands.

As far as day-to-day use is concerned, Linux is no different from most commercially available Unix systems, which means that a user may comfortably switch between the two. To a large extent, this is due to the fact that Linux complies with the POSIX standards, which unite diverse characteristics of existing standards and are independent of any manufacturer. As a result, there are often fewer differences between Linux and a POSIX-compliant Unix than between two Unix systems.

Principal characteristics of Linux

Linux has the following characteristics in common with Unix:
− multi-tasking
− multi-user
− multi-processing
− multi-platform
− 32 and 64 bit versions

Unlike Unix, the Linux source code is available, which has greatly contributed to its diffusion and improvement. This, incidentally, used to be the case for Unix as well; from the beginning of its history, until the breaking-up of AT&T.

Apart from its technical characteristics, perhaps the most attractive aspect of Linux is its design philosophy. Each command is a tool which does only one thing, but does it well. This makes for efficient products. Moreover, this modular design allows you to connect commands together in order to answer specific needs, precisely and efficiently. To obtain this performance, a certain amount of time must be spent in understanding the overall logic. Once this is done, anything is possible.

A. What is Linux ?

When you log in to the system, by entering your username and password, you immediately access the file system, which is a set of files organized into a hierarchical structure.

As a user, your status with respect to the each of these files can be one of the following:
— either you are the file owner, in which case you can do anything with the file
— or, you belong to the owner group for this file
— or, you are neither owner nor do you belong to the owner group

In the two last cases, your actions on the file are limited by the permissions granted by the file owner.

The concepts of ownership, owner groups and access permissions are fundamental to Linux. For a system administrator, application of these concepts represents the first step towards system security, and many functioning and security problems arise from maladjusted ownership options and access permissions.

(kernel version 2.0 à 2.2)

Chapter 1

To work with the system, you must be able to communicate with it. On Unix, this is done using a program called the *Shell* which surrounds the kernel and provides the interface with the user. There are a number of Unix shells. The three most common are the *Bourne-shell*, the *C-shell* and the *Korn-shell*. Usually, Linux uses the *Bash* (Bourne Again Shell). This shell is covered by the GNU copyleft. The Bash bears many similarities to the *Bourne-shell* and the *Korn-shell*, and has some characteristics in common with the *C-shell*.

Each of these shells has specific characteristics and function modes. You need to know at least one of these shells to really feel at home with the system.

In this book, *Bash*, the standard Linux *shell* will be covered in two stages. First, we will set out the essential concepts you need to understand to be able to use the system properly. Following this, the interactive aspects of some of the more advanced characteristics will be presented.

Although this book does not concern Unix directly, the differences between the two main Unix versions (System V and *BSD*) will be described in order to show where Linux fits in.

Overview

Using Linux

B. Purpose of this book

For every operating system, there are one or more people in charge of its administration and functioning, and there are the day to day users. In general, users do not have access to administration commands. However, they do have access to a vast range of utilities that they must understand in order to carry out their work.

This book is a presentation of the basic principles of using the Linux system (the same principles as for any Unix system) and its most useful commands. It is not, however, an exhaustive presentation of the 600 or so commands available, many of which are too specific for every-day use. In addition, this book does not cover the complete set of options for each command. There are two reasons for this:
— First, amongst the options for each command, some are very specialized and sometimes not portable from one system to another. This is not specific to Linux, the same problem exists with all Unix systems.
— Second, presenting the complete set of options for the whole range of commands would have been the equivalent of the on-line help offered by Linux. This is not the objective of this book, which aims at providing the fundamentals of using Linux and allowing the user to gain sufficient autonomy.

This book covers the most frequently used, and portable commands. This choice ensures that you will be able to work and feel at home on all Linux or Unix systems. However, some commands or options specific to Linux will be presented. When this is the case it will be clearly indicated.

(kernel version 2.0 à 2.2)

Chapter 1

Page 13

...terfaces for the follo-
...ty. It is essential to
...Unix systems, even
...ns. A knowledge of
...seful understanding
...commands tend to
...dard commands is
...cal interfaces.
...tem design. In fact,
...ential component of
...ossible to use the
...phical interfaces are
...servers, so as not

Overview

Using Linux

↓ *personal notes* ↓

Chapter 2
Linux file system hierarchy

A. **The path concept** 17
   1. Absolute paths and relative paths 17

B. **Presenting the Filesystem Hierarchy Standard** 18

On some operating systems such as MS-DOS, MacOs or the Windows series (95, 98, NT), each physical disk drive (floppy, hard disk or CD-ROM) has its own file hierarchy or logical organization. In addition, when you want to access a file or a directory you must specify the name of the disk drive on which it is stored.

On Linux systems, the number, type and physical organisation of storage peripherals does not concern the user. The user works with only one file hierarchy, made up of several levels. For a long time, the composition of these levels differed from one version to another, with no standard for directory names or contents. Today, a new hierarchy called the *Filesystem Hierarchy Standard* has been designed that is slowly and progressively being adopted, sometimes introducing a certain amount of confusion. This standard is the Linux equivalent of the Unix *New Filesystem Layout*. There is a lot of similarity between them, which indicates a real convergence between Unix and Linux.

The first objective of this new hierarchy was to clearly differentiate between commands working with configuration files, and those working with variable files (spools, administrative, logging) for which the size frequently varies. The commands themselves are divided up into different directories according to whether they are available to all users or whether they are more specifically reserved for the system administrator.

(kernel version 2.0 à 2.2)

A. The path concept

1. Absolute paths and relative paths

As the filesystem hierarchy is organized on several levels, it is essential to have a means of locating a particular file or directory. The *path* refers to the series of levels which must be followed to access the required item, the names of successive levels being separated by the / character. The **absolute path** refers to the path starting from the **root directory**. This is the "top" directory in the hierarchy, the parent of all the other directories, either directly or indirectly. The **relative path** refers to a path starting from another level. By convention, the root directory has no name and any path for which the first character is a slash (/) is an absolute path. If it does not begin with a /, it is a relative path starting from the current directory.

For a relative path, you may need to go up rather than down. You can do this using a special notation (..). When it is created, each directory contains two subdirectories called "." and "..". The former refers to the directory containing it, whilst the latter refers to the parent directory of the directory containing it. To go up a level from the current directory, the path must begin with a "..". Examples will be given on the section covering the **cd** command.

B. Presenting the Filesystem Hierarchy Standard

This section describes the principal directories of this hierarchy's first level.

As the hierarchy covers the entire system, it has only one root containing a number of first-level directories.

- **/bin** This directory contains most commands that are generally available to all users
- **/boot** This directory contains the programs and data files necessary to boot the system. Its contents have not yet been standardized and may vary from one distribution to another.
- **/dev** The files contained in this directory are said to be "special files" in the sense that they form the interfaces to every device that the Linux kernel is configured to support.
- **/etc** For a long time, this directory was used to accommodate administration commands and system configuration files. Now, the new standards dedicate this directory to system configuration files and subdirectories. The administration commands have been moved to /**sbin**. However, even in some recent versions of Unix, this migration is not completely finished: links to local commands in /**sbin** still remain in /**etc** so that these commands continue to be accessible from this directory.
- **/home** This new directory is provided to contain user home directories, for use when the user logs in to the system.

(kernel version 2.0 à 2.2)

/lib This directory contains essential shared libraries and kernel modules. Less essential libraries or those specific to a particular program or application are stored in **/usr/lib**.

/lost+found It can happen, albeit rarely, that files are lost following a system crash or a software error. These files can be retrieved using the **fsck** program which saves them in this directory.

/mnt This directory is a mount point for temporarily mounted file systems (on remote computers, floppies...)

/proc This directory appeared relatively recently in the Unix world, but it has been in existence for a long time already on Linux. The files it contains do not exist physically and are used for virtual storage of data for active processes. Access to this data is provided by a set of file-processing system calls.

/tmp Temporary files are stored in this directory by the kernel and also by some users. These files exist for very short periods. This directory is usually cleared by the system, either at boot time, or periodically, if the system is not booted relatively frequently.

/usr This directory contains commands and files which are not essential for booting the system. It is made up of a number of subdirectories:
- **adm** provides access to system logging and accounting files
- **bin** contains most user commands
- **include** contains include-files necessary for program compiling

- **lib** contains objects and static data including executable code for programs and subsystems
- **man** contains manual pages
- **sbin** contains system administration commands which are not essential to boot the system.
- **tmp** is used for temporary files

The reasons for this dual structure are mainly historical. They date from a time when disk capacities did not allow the storage of the complete hierarchy on one disk. It was therefore split up into two parts, one of which was located on the main disk, in order to boot the system. The other occupied one or more secondary disks, accessible from the /**usr** directory. This division between the **root** directory and /**usr** is no longer necessary with modern disks.

/var This directory contains the set of files which vary in size during normal system running. This is the case for system logging and accounting files, which are stored in /**var/log** and pointed to by the /**usr/adm** directory. /**var** also contains the spool directory for printing and other queued work. It contains one subdirectory per printer, the mail subdirectory accommodating user mailboxes and an additional temporary subdirectory.

The above is merely a simplified presentation of a hierarchical structure that can be found on all Unix systems. Beyond these first levels, the hierarchy tends to vary considerably from one system to another, to suit the needs of the site in question.

In summary then, Linux organizes its files and directories into a single hierarchy structured on several levels. The next step is to learn how to refer to the items of this hierarchy, or in other words, how to indicate their path.

(kernel version 2.0 à 2.2)

A path is the list of directories you need to follow to reach the required file or directory, with path elements being separated by the slash (/) character.

There are two types of path:
- an absolute path begins in the hierarchical root and leads to the required file or directory. As the root has no name, absolute paths always begin with a / character. For example, to access the **bin** directory in the **local** directory, itself being in the **usr** directory, the absolute path would be:

```
/usr/local/bin
```

- a relative path begins in the current directory (this is whichever directory the user is in when the command is executed). For example, suppose that the user is in the **/usr** directory and wishes to refer to the **bin** directory used in the above example. In this case the following relative path could be used:

```
local/bin
```

As the **local** directory is contained directly in the current directory (**/usr**), the relative path is simpler.

Up until now, we have considered only descending paths, i.e. each successive element of the path was contained in the preceding element. For example, for the path **/usr/local/bin**, the **bin** directory is contained in the **local** directory, which is contained in the **usr** directory, which is contained in the **root**.

Now, supposing you are in the **/usr/local/lib** directory. To access the same **/usr/local/bin** directory relatively, you must first move up a level so as to move down again to the **bin** directory. You can do this because each directory contains an item that points to the parent directory. This item is called "..". So, the relative path to bin would be:
```
../bin
```

This indicates that you wish to move up one level then move down to **bin**. It must be noted that you can move up as many levels as you need to.

↓ personal notes ↓

(kernel version 2.0 à 2.2)

Chapter 3

Defining users and groups

A. Users 24

B. Groups 26

A. Users

As a multi-user system, Linux must be able to distinguish between one user and another, and provide them with customised access facilities.

To this end each user is assigned a certain number of characteristics when the user account is created. These characteristics are as follows:

Login user name

This name is used only when you log in to the system. After you have logged in, the system works with a user identification number (UID). The login name is handy though, as it is easier to remember a name than a number. This name must not contain more than 8 characters. Every Linux system has a super-user account, called **root** by default.

Password

This is a character string that allows the system to check whether or not the user is genuine. The idea is that, while it may be easy to find out the names of the system's users, it must not be possible to find out their passwords. Passwords must be chosen carefully and must never be written down. A password can be up to 8 characters in length (some systems have extended this maximum size to 16 characters). As a general rule, a password should contain at least 5 characters consisting of upper case and lower case letters and punctuation marks. This makes it harder for the programs designed to "crack" system passwords. In addition, password ageing utilities are available, which force users to change their passwords at an interval decided by the system administrator.

(kernel version 2.0 à 2.2)

UID - user identifiers

This is a unique number assigned to each user by the system so that it can distinguish between one user and another. It is according to their UID and not to their login name that users will be assigned access permissions to files and directories. The UID of the root account is 0. Similarly, super-user permissions are not granted because of the name **root**, but because the super-user UID is 0.

GID - group identifiers

A group is a set of users who share files and/or directories. Each user belongs to at least one group. This is the user's primary group, which is the group associated with other login characteristics such as the user name.

Home directory

This is the user's current directory immediately after login.

Login program

This is the program that is started when the user logs in to the system. It is generally a shell, providing the user with an interface to the system. When this program is stopped, the user is automatically logged out of the system. In fact, the login program must stop for logout to occur.

The set of attributes for each user is stored in a basic Unix file called **/etc/passwd**. Each entry in this file describes an account and is made up of a number of fields separated by colons (:). Each field contains a characteristic of the account. A supplementary field is provided to contain information on the user. This field is not used by the system and is generally empty nowadays.

Here is a sample extract from this file :

```
root:7NQd1ECmIJK9Y:0:0:root,,,:/root:/bin/ksh
bin:*:1:1:bin,,,:/bin:
daemon:*:2:2:daemon,,,:/sbin:
adm:*:3:4:adm,,,:/var/adm:
lp:*:4:7:lp,,,:/var/spool/lpd:
...
nobody:*:65535:100:nobody,,,:/dev/null:
sgbd:*:507:105::/home/sgbd:/bin/ksh
webroot:*:1050:110:Web Administrator:
/home/webmaster:/bin/ksh
webuser:*:1051:110:Web User:
/home/webmaster:/bin/false
squid:*:1052:20:Proxy Administrator:
/usr/local/squid:/bin/ksh
```

Note the second field in the first line of this file. This is the root password after encryption by the system. It is *not* the password as **root** would enter it!

B. Groups

Groups are defined in the **/etc/group** file. Its structure is similar to that of the **/etc/passwd** file. Each entry defines a group and is made up of a number of fields separated by colons (:). The following fields are present:
— group name
— group password (this field is often empty as it is not always used nowadays)
— group identifier (**GID**)
— a list of all the users that are members of the group, separated by commas (,).

(kernel version 2.0 à 2.2)

Chapter 3

Here is a sample extract from this file :

```
root::0:root,system,squid
bin::1:root,bin,daemon
daemon::2:root,bin,daemon
sys::3:root,bin,adm
adm::4:root,adm,daemon
tty::5:
disk::6:root,adm
lp::7:lp
mem::8:
kmem::9:system
wheel::10:root,system
floppy::11:root,system,webroot
mail::12:mail
news::13:news
uucp::14:uucp,system
man::15:man
operator::16:root,system
users::100:games,system
sgbd::105:system
shadow::111:root
web::110:
squid::20:root,system
```

Linux has adopted the BSD group concept. Under Unix System V, a user could belong to only one group at a time, whereas under BSD and Linux, you can belong to several groups simultaneously. You have a primary group which is the one assigned in the **/etc/passwd** file and you can belong to a number of secondary groups as specified in the **/etc/group** file. The great advantage of belonging to several groups is that you can have immediate access to files in different groups as soon as permission is given for the file in question. Whereas, under System V, you had to change groups explicitly to access a file in another group, under Linux and BSD you can access these files directly, without having to modify your primary group.

The difference between primary and secondary groups can be explained as follows: when you create a file it is assigned to your primary group. To create a file and assign it to another group, you can do one of two things:
– change your primary group before creating the file
– create the file and then assign it to another group

The first action can be done using **newgrp**, whereas the second uses the **chgrp** command. These commands will be presented in the next chapter.

(kernel version 2.0 à 2.2)

Chapter 4

Logging in and entering your first commands

A.	Login procedure	30
B.	General command presentation	32
C.	Entering more than one command	34
	1. Unconditional execution	34
	2. Conditional execution	34

Using Linux

A. Login procedure

Equipped with this basic information, you are now ready to look at logging in to Unix in general and to Linux in particular.

For the purposes of this section, it is assumed that the login will be made on a serial terminal.

Once the terminal has been switched on, a screen appears which may look like the following:

```
Welcome to merlin.dorset.uk (tty2)

merlin login:
```

The contents of this message may vary from one system to another. Part of this message is defined by the system administrator in **/etc/issue**.

The most important part of this message is the "login:" string which invites you to identify yourself with your user name. Once the user name has been entered and confirmed with the [Enter] key, the "Password:" string appears inviting you to enter your password. You must be careful here as no echo is returned to the screen for security reasons: not even neutral characters are returned as this would reveal the length of the password, which would provide a first clue to its contents.

After the user name and password have been entered, the system verifies the validity of these two elements and either accepts or refuses the login. If one of the two is erroneous, the message "Login incorrect" is displayed, and it is left to the user to find the error. Again, this is done for security reasons, so as not to help intruders by indicating that the error is in the username or the password.

(kernel version 2.0 à 2.2)

Once the login has been accepted a message appears which may be similar to the following:

```
2 failures since last login. Last was 10:37:03 on ttyp3.
Last login: Wed Feb 10 10:11:01 on ttyp2 from arthur.dorset..
No mail.
$
```

The first line indicates the number of unsuccessful logins since the last successful one and the second line shows when and where you logged in last. This information gives you an indication of any intrusions or attempted intrusions onto your account. The third line indicates if you have received any mail.

The system administrator may wish to inform users about the system, for example to warn of any planned downtimes. To do this, the administrator enters the information into the **/etc/motd** (message of the day) file. The contents of this file are systematically displayed upon login.

The **$** character is the system **prompt** indicating that the system is ready for you to enter a command. A **$** prompt appears for all users except for the system administrator for whom the **#** character is used. In fact, you are not interacting with the system here, but with the **shell**, which acts as the intermediary between you and the system.
The *Bourne-Shell*, the *Korn-Shell* and the *Bash* shell use the **$** prompt for the general users, whereas the C-Shell uses the **%** character. However, this is only the default character for the prompt: you can modify the prompt character as you require. It is stored in a variable that is local to the *shell* of each user.

You are now ready to start entering commands, but first we will examine the overall syntax of the principal Linux commands.

B. General command presentation

Every command has a name which is usually quite short and in the form of an abbreviation such as **cp** for copy, **sed** for stream editor...

For some commands, the name may be entered alone, as for the **id** command which displays information on your account. Other commands require one or more arguments providing further information.

The great thing about the commands is that they do only one thing at a time, and they do it well: they do not attempt to do something else that is executed efficiently by another command. To execute a complex task well, all you have to do is to combine together several commands. Thus, you can consider commands as being so many building blocks to be put together according to your needs. This results in command lines. These may appear a little esoteric to the beginner, for example:

```
ls *.new | sed "s/\(.*\)\.new$/mv '&' '\1.old'/" | sh
```

This command takes all the filenames in the current directory with a .new extension and transforms these extensions to .old. The difficulty in understanding the meaning of such a command is equaled only by the power it provides. In fact, the only limit to the construction of commands is the imagination of the user. You can do practically anything, and often in several ways: for example, the above command could have been written as follows:

```
ls *.new | sed "s/\(.*\)\.new$/\1/" | \
xargs -i mv {}.new {}.old
```

Although they are programmed to fulfil a fairly limited role, most commands offer options that allow you to make very shrewd adjustments to their action.

(kernel version 2.0 à 2.2)

An option is specified by a letter preceded by a dash (-), as for the **-a** option of the **ls** command:

```
ls -a
```

The role of the dash is merely to introduce the option. Moreover, you can string together several options after just one dash, although you can use one dash per option if you prefer. In addition, the order of the options is generally unimportant for most commands, so that the following three commands are all equivalent:

```
ls -a -l
```

or

```
ls -al
```

or

```
ls -la
```

It must be noted, however, that any options must appear after the command name and before the arguments. Here is a summary of the overall syntax of Unix commands:

command for commands which do not necessa-
[options] rily require arguments.

command for commands which require one or
[options] more arguments. Note the convention
arguments that all syntax items appearing between square brackets [] are optional,
whereas all syntax items not appearing between square brackets must be
provided.

You can also string together several commands on the same line. By this means you can avoid waiting for the first command to finish before starting the second, then waiting for the second command to finish before starting the third...

C. Entering more than one command

There are two ways of stringing commands together: by specifying unconditional execution, and by specifying conditional execution.

1. Unconditional execution

Unconditional execution of a string of commands means that each command will be executed irrespective of whether the preceding command was successful or not. This is done by separating the command with a semi-colon (;).

```
# date;whoami
Fri Feb 12 09:54:36 MET 1999
root
```

In a single line, the user has requested execution of the **date** and the **whoami** commands. The first command displays the current date and time whilst the second displays the login name of the user (**root** in this case).

This technique simply allows you to string together several command lines into one.

2. Conditional execution

You may wish to start a second command only if the first command was successful. In this case, you can use the **&&** operator as a command separator instead of the semi-colon.

```
# date && whoami
Fri Feb 12 09:54:36 MET 1999
root
```

For this example, the result is the same as for the unconditional execution, as the **date** command did not encounter any problems.

(kernel version 2.0 à 2.2)

Chapter 4

However, you may wish to execute a second command only if the first command fails and not if it is successful. For this purpose you can use the || operator.

```
# date || whoami
Fri Feb 12 09:54:36 MET 1999
```

In this case, as the first command was successful, the second command was not executed.

Here are a few commands which provide you with user information:

➔ **logname**

This simple command returns the name of the user who invoked it.

```
$ logname
soloa
```

*The **whoami** command fulfils an identical function.*

➔ **id**

supplies fuller information on the current user:

```
$ id
uid=504(system) gid=100(users) groups=100(users)
,10(wheel)
```

The command displays the **uid** with the username, then the **gid** and the primary group name, followed by the list of secondary groups to which the user belongs.

➔ **tty**

displays the name of the special **/dev** file that provides the interface with the terminal on which the user logged in:

```
$ tty
/dev/tty1
```

→ uname

Returns the name of the operating system:

```
$ uname
Linux
```

You can modify the output of this command with a number of options.

Here is a selection of those most commonly used:

- **-m** displays the type of machine hardware (generally the type of CPU board)
- **-n** displays the name by which the system is known on the Internet.
- **-r** displays the operating system release number
- **-s** displays the name of the operating system (this is the option by default)
- **-v** displays the date and time of the kernel construction (version).
- **-a** equivalent to all the above options (**-mnrsv**)

```
$ uname -m
i586
$ uname -n
merlin
$ uname -r
2.2.1
$ uname -s
Linux
$ uname -v
#11 Mon Feb 8 18:51:22 MET 1999
$ uname -a
Linux merlin 2.2.1 #11 Mon Feb 8 18:51:22
MET 1999 i586 unknown
```

(kernel version 2.0 à 2.2)

➔ **who**

displays the list of users currently logged in to the system:

```
$ who
root      tty0      Feb 21 23:41
soloa     ttyp1     Feb 22 09:32 (:0.0)
system    ttyp3     Feb 23 11:36 (arthur.dorset.)
```

By default, the following information is displayed:
– names of the users
– special terminal file name
– login date and time
– the origin of the connection
  In the above example, the empty field indicates a local connection on the system administrators terminal. (:0.0) is also a local connection but on a graphic terminal, whereas the indication (arthur.dorset.) indicates a remote connection from the arthur.dorset.uk machine.

One of the most useful options of **who** is **-H** which displays column headings:

```
$ who -H
USER      LINE      LOGIN-TIME    FROM
root      tty0      Feb 21 23:41
soloa     ttyp1     Feb 22 09:32 (:0.0)
system    ttyp3     Feb 23 11:36 (arthur.dorset.)
```

Here are a few other useful options:

- **-m** acts like the **whoami** command, displaying only the line concerning the user who invoked the command
- **-i, -u** displays terminal idle time. A dot (.) indicates that there was activity in the last minute and **old** indicates that there has been no activity for over 24 hours.
- **-q** lists the names and numbers of logged-in users.

-w indicates whether or not each user listed accepts messages sent using the **write** command (this command is covered in Chapter 14, Principle Linux commands). This is indicated in the second column: a **+** means that messages are accepted by the user concerned, and a **-** means that they are refused.

```
$ who -Hm
        USER       LINE    LOGIN-TIME      FROM
merlin!system      ttyp3   Feb 23 11:36   (arthur.dorset.)
$ who am i
merlin!system      ttyp3   Feb 23 11:36   (arthur.dorset.)
$ who -Hi
USER    LINE      LOGIN-TIME      IDLE    FROM
root    tty0      Feb 21 23:41    01:00
soloa   ttyp1     Feb 22 09:32    01:01   (:0.0)
system  ttyp3     Feb 23 11:36      .     (arthur.dorset.)
$ who -Hq
root soloa system
# users=3
$ who -Hw
USER    MESG LINE    LOGIN-TIME      FROM
root     -   tty0    Feb 21 23:41
soloa    -   ttyp1   Feb 22 09:32   (:0.0)
system   -   ttyp3   Feb 23 11:36   (arthur.dorset.)
```

➔ **passwd**

allows you to change your password. There are several versions of this command, some of which allow password selection rules to be laid down to avoid password choices that could compromise system security.

After you have invoked the command you are asked first to confirm your old password. This is done to prevent another person taking advantage of your temporary absence.

Then, you are asked to enter the new password. Following this, as the password is not echoed to the screen, you are asked to input the new password a second time to check for any typing errors.

(kernel version 2.0 à 2.2)

In the following example, the command has a number of internal rules, so that passwords must:
– contain from 5 to 8 characters
– be composed of a combination of upper case and lower case letters and numbers

In addition, the command rejects choices judged to be too simple. Although the verification it makes is very quick, it avoids passwords that may be guessed too easily.

```
$ passw
Changing password for system
Old password:
Enter the new password (minimum of 5, maximum of
8 characters)
Please use a combination of upper and lower case
letters and numbers.
New password:
Too simple, try again
New password:
Re-enter new password:
Password changed successfully
```

The most common version (shadow password) allows a password ageing mechanism to be used. The various parameters can be adjusted so as to:
– define the minimum number of days for which a password is valid, so that modification attempts before the end of this period will be rejected
– define the maximum number of days for which a password is valid, so that you are obliged to change your password after the end of this period
– lock an account after a certain number of failed connection attempts
– lock an account a certain number of days after expiry of the password
– set the number of days on which warning messages are displayed prior to the expiry of the password (see example below)
– lock an account automatically on a certain date.

```
Linux 2.2.1 (merlin.dorset.uk)   (ttyp4)



merlin login: soloa
Password:
Welcome to Linux 2.2.1.
Last login: Wed Feb 24 11:18:13 on ttyp4
from arthur.dorset..
Your password will expire tomorrow.
No mail.
$
```

You can obtain information on your password using the **-S** option of the **passwd** command:

```
$ passwd -S
soloa P 08/05/97 0 10000 0 0
```

The following information is obtained:
— name of the user
— status of the user's account: **P** if the password is active, **NP** if the password has been deactivated, **L** if the account is locked
— the date the password was last modified
— the age (in days) the password must have before it can be changed
— the maximum age of the password (in days) after which it must be changed
— the number of days on which warning messages are displayed prior to the expiry of the password
— the number of days which can elapse after password expiry before the account is automatically locked

(kernel version 2.0 à 2.2)

Chapter 4

→ newgrp

This command allows you to create a new session by modifying your primary group. This is useful if you need to access, or possibly create, files in a group other than your primary group. As you are not making a fresh connection, the session is created without you having to enter your password, by stacking shells. This means that the shell in which **newgrp** is invoked starts a new command shell with the primary group being that specified in the **newgrp** command argument. This is illustrated in the following example, where the prompt indicates the current command number. Here, command 10 executes the command **newgrp sgbd** which opens a new shell, starting with command 1. When the session is closed this number reverts to command 11 of the original shell.

```
[9]-system(merlin)~:id
uid=504(system) gid=100(users) groups=100(users),105(sgbd)
[10]-system(merlin)~:newgrp sgbd
[1]-system(merlin)~:id
uid=504(system) gid=105(sgbd) groups=100(users),105(sgbd)
[2]-system(merlin)~:exit
exit
[11]-system(merlin)~:id
uid=504(system) gid=100(users) groups=100(users),105(sgbd)
```

Logging in and entering your first commands

Using Linux

↓ personal notes ↓

Chapter 5

User owners and owner groups

A. Users and owner groups 44

B. Changing owner and group for a file 45

With respect to each file or directory, Linux has three different categories of user:
- the user is the owner of the file or directory
- the user is a member of the owner group of the file or directory
- the user is neither the owner, nor a member of the owner group, of the file or directory

As we shall see in the next chapter, the access permissions to each file or directory are managed according to these three possible identities.

A. Users and owner groups

When you create a file or a directory you become its owner. However, the group ownership by default depends on the ownership system.

In the case of the BSD system, the owner group of the file or directory is the group of the directory in which it is created.

In the case of System V, the owner group of the file or directory is the group of the user who created it.

A BSD type of functioning is emulated when the group set-ID is turned on. In this case, the default owner group of all files created in this directory will be that of this directory. This is extended access permission.

By default, Linux functions like System V in this respect. It is, however, possible to emulate BSD functioning (as this aspect concerns system administration, it is covered in our Linux Administration book).

(kernel version 2.0 à 2.2)

B. Changing owner and group for a file

For Linux, BSD and certain other Unix systems, file ownership can be changed only by the system administrator. Changing ownership is a convenient technique to manage disk space usage quotas. By no longer being the owner of some of your files, you can free up some of your disk space quota. This is particularly suitable for managing files for which you are the owner involuntarily. It must be noted that the System V family also reserves the **chmod** command (which changes file access permissions) for **root** when disk space quotas are set.

The command to use is the same as for System V:

```
chown NEW_OWNER FILE
```

However, **chown** accepts the following syntax, which allows you to modify the group.

```
chown NEW_OWNER[.[NEW_GROUP]] FILE
```

There are three possible actions:
chown OWNER
modifies only the owner of the file.
chown OWNER.GROUP
modifies the owner and the group to which the file belongs.
chown OWNER.
modifies user and group ownership of the file: the owner group is the primary group of the new owner.

The owner of a file can change the file's owner group, provided that the owner is a member of the new group.

The command is as follows:

```
chgrp NEW_GROUP FILE
```

(kernel version 2.0 à 2.2)

Chapter 6

Permission to access files and directories

A. Access permissions for files 48

B. Directory permissions 50

C. Modifying access permissions 51

D. Extended access permissions 54

A. Access permissions for files

For each file there is:
— read permission (r)
— write permission (w)
— execute permission (x)

Each of these permissions can be set for any of the following:
— the owner of the file
— the owner group of the file
— other users

To display permissions for a file use:
```
ls -l FILE
```

and for a directory, use:
```
ls -ld DIRECTORY
```

This command provides information on the file whose name is passed as an argument, thanks to the presence of the **-l** option.

These permissions can be set using symbolic and octal notations:

	owner	group	other
symbolic permissions	r w x	r - x	r - x
binary permissions	1 1 1	1 0 1	1 0 1
octal permissions	7	5	5

As the above table illustrates, each permission is represented by a bit which is 1 when the permission is set and 0 when it is not set. From left to right each set of three bits, go from most significant to least significant.

Each file acquires default permissions when it is created. These permissions are called the **file creation mode mask**.

(kernel version 2.0 à 2.2)

Chapter 6

To display the value of the file-creation mode mask, use **umask** which is a shell built-in command.

```
$ umask
022
```

The value of these default permissions is obtained by subtracting the mask from the maximal permissions value. A file has maximal permissions when it is has read and write permission. Execute permission is never set when a file is created except in the case of a compiler objet file.

	owner	group	other
maximal symbolic permissions on creation	r w -	r w -	r w -
maximal octal permissions on creation	6	6	6
maximal binary permissions on creation	1 1 0	1 1 0	1 1 0
binary mask	0 0 0	1 1 0	1 1 0
octal mask	0	6	6
binary permission granted	1 1 0	0 0 0	0 0 0
octal permission granted	6	0	0
symbolic permission granted	r w -	- - -	- - -

Thus, to calculate the granted permissions: granted permissions = maxmal permissions - mask. For example, owner granted permission = 110 - 000 = 6 - 0 = 6 octal.

To modify the value of a mask, pass the new mask value as an argument to the **umask** command.

```
$ umask 066
$ umask
066
```

The **umask** command of the Bash shell allows you to use symbolic notation.

Permission to access files and directories

Using Linux

B. Directory permissions

A directory has the same types of access permissions as a file. Although access permissions for files are fairly easy to understand, those for directories need a little explanation.

Permission	Meaning
r	The contents of the directory can be displayed. This permission is necessary for the **ls** command, and for the shell, to set up search criteria for file names. To limit the visibility of directory contents, this permission can be reset to zero for "other" access.
w	The contents of the directory can be modified. This permission allows the user to create or delete files and directories contained in the directory. The ability to delete an individual item in a directory with **w** pemission is independent of the access permissions for this item.
x	The name of the directory can appear in a path. This permission is necessary to be able to execute, for example, the **cd** command on this directory. All the items contained in a directory are completely locked (inaccessible) if this permission is not set.

The default permissions set for a directory when it is created are determined in the same way as for a file, except that the maximal read, write and execute permissions for all types of user are 777 in octal notation and rwxrwxrwx in symbolic notation. As there is only one mask, its value must be determined so as to define the default permissions for files and directories. In this way, a mask of 077 allows the owner to create files and directories, with no permission granted to group and other users.

(kernel version 2.0 à 2.2)

C. Modifying access permissions

We have just seen that each file and directory is created with default access permissions. For various reasons, a user may need to modify them. This is done using the **chmod** command, for which the syntax is as follows:

```
chmod NEW-PERMISSIONS FILES(S)
```

The new permissions may be given in octal notation as absolute new values, irrespective of the old values. Alternatively, new permissions may be given in symbolic notation, in which case it is possible to add and remove permissions with respect to their old values (in addition to applying absolute permission values).

> *Only the file owner and the system administrator can modify the access permissions of a file.*

Symbolic notation is used as follows:

```
who how what
```

who the recipients of the new permissions. They can be the owner, the group or others. The following notation is used to identify them:
– **u** (user) for the owner
– **g** for the group
– **o** for others

These symbols can be strung together to specify several user types. To indicate user, group and other the letter **a** (all) can be used instead of **ugo**.

how This is the operator to be used for assigning the permissions. There are three possible operators:

= to assign only those permissions specified irrespective of the old values.

+ to add values to existing permissions

- to remove permissions

what These are the permissions to be taken into account, for which there are three possibilities:

r for read permission
w for write permission
x for execute permission

These values can be strung together as for the permission recipients. For example, **rw** assigns read and write permissions.

You can also use a short format:

u to use the permissions of the owner
g to use the permissions of the group
o to use the permissions of other
X sets execution permission if this has already been set for another type of user, otherwise it is ignored. For example g+X will set execution permission for the group only if the owner or other already have this permission set.

(kernel version 2.0 à 2.2)

Chapter 6

Several different symbolic modes can be assigned by separating them with a comma (,) as shown in the fourth example below:

Examples:

```
$ ls -l mbox
-rw-------   1 soloa    users     2200 Jan 21 09:25 mbox
$ chmod 644 mbox
$ ls -l mbox
-rw-r--r--   1 soloa    users     2200 Jan 21 09:25 mbox
$ chmod ug+w,o-r mbox
$ ls -l mbox
-rw-rw----   1 soloa    users     2200 Jan 21 09:25 mbox
$ chmod g=r mbox
$ ls -l mbox
-rw-r-----   1 soloa    users     2200 Jan 21 09:25 mbox
$ chmod =
----------   1 soloa    users     2200 Jan 21 09:25 mbox
```

D. Extended access permissions

There are three other permissions that can be given. The **SUID (set user ID)** permission, the **SGID (set group ID)** permission and the **Sticky Bit**, which are set respectively using **s** for user, **s** for group and **t** for either owner or other.

Here is the role of each of these permissions:

SUID is useful only for an executable file. In the absence of this permission, every command runs with the identity of the user who invoked it. This limits the action of the command to files for which the user has the required rights. With the **SUID** permission applied, the command will be executed under the identity of its owner, which grants the user particular access permissions (those of the file owner) for execution of the file. The classic example of this is the **passwd** command. In fact, no user except **root** has the permission to modify the password file. However, this is what every user does to change passwords. This is possible because the **/usr/bin/passwd** file has **SUID** permission:

```
$ ls -l /usr/bin/passwd
-rwsr-xr-x   1 root    root     30476 Feb  6 14:03 /usr/bin/passwd
```

As has already been mentioned, this special permission is of interest only in relation to execution permission. As these two permissions share the same permission position and only **SUID** is visible when set, it was decided to use an **s** (lower-case) to indicate the simultaneous setting of these two permissions and an **S** (upper-case) to indicate that the **SUID** permission has been set but not the execution permission.

(kernel version 2.0 à 2.2)

Chapter 6

```
$ su -
Password:
# chmod a-x /usr/bin/passwd
# ls -l /usr/bin/passwd
-rwSr--r--   1 root    root      30476 Feb  6 14:03/
usr/bin/passwd
# passwd
su: /usr/bin/passwd: Permission denied
```

SGID for a file has a similar meaning to that of **SUID** permission, but this time concerning the group. **SGID** is useful to extend certain permissions, without endangering the security of the system should the program have execution problems (these aspects are beyond the scope of this book). For a directory, this permission modifies the group assignments for new files. As has already been mentioned, by default, when a file is created it belongs to the same group as the user who created it. When a directory has **SGID** permission, all files created in it will belong to the same group as the directory and not to that of their owner. This technique allows several users working on the same project to share files simply by being members of the group of a common directory. They do not need to have the same primary group.

The same convention as for **SUID** is used to indicate whether or not execution permission is set when the **SGID** permission is set.

Sticky bit is a permission that fulfils two roles according to whether it is applied to an executable file or to a directory. However, it is hardly ever applied to files any more because of increasingly rapid disk access. When set on an executable file, the sticky bit requests the system to keep this executable in memory ready for future use, so as not to lose time re-loading it from disk.

Nowadays, the sticky bit is mainly used with directories, such as **/tmp** for example. As has already been mentioned, **/tmp** is a common directory in which everyone can store temporarily any file they like. However, as everyone can write to this directory, they can also delete any file they like, even those belonging to other users. This negates the benefit of the common directory. This problem is solved using the **sticky bit**, a special permission that authorizes you to delete files in a directory only if you are the owner of the directory.

The **sticky bit** permission uses the "other" execution position. Similarly to the convention used by the SUID and SGID permissions, a **t** (lower-case) indicates the simultaneous setting of the **sticky bit** and execution permission, whilst a **T** (upper-case) indicates that the sticky bit permission has been set, but not the execution permission.

```
$ ls -ld /tmp
drwxrwxrwt   4 root     root      3072 Feb 25 10:35 /tmp
```

(kernel version 2.0 à 2.2)

Chapter 7

The Bash Shell

A.	Overview	58
B.	Entering commands	59
C.	Editing a command	60
D.	Aliases	63
	1. Defining an alias	64
	2. Listing current aliases	65
	3. Deleting an alias	66
E.	History and command substitutions	66
	1. Displaying the command history	67
	2. Recalling and editing a command	70
	3. Immediate substitution	72
	4. Using C-shell type history commands	73
F.	Environment variables	74
G.	Shell built-in commands	76
H.	Meta-characters and special characters	89
I.	Parsing the command line	92
J.	Initializing the environment	93
K.	Customizing the prompt	95

Using Linux

A. Overview

The *Bourne shell* appeared in 1976 and is a standard Unix shell. The *C-shell* was developed by the BSD branch with a different syntax (similar to that of C language) that is incompatible with that of the *Bourne shell*. The *C-shell* introduced a number of useful features such as command history, filename completion, alias management and job control.

The Korn-shell has been the standard for Unix System V since version 4. This is a re-write of the Bourne shell by David Korn. It introduced a number of important extensions, some of which came from the C-shell, whilst ensuring backwards compatibility with the Bourne shell.

Since the end of the 1980's, two other shells have appeared, both freely distributable: **tcsh** and **bash**.

The **tsch** shell is an extension of the C-shell. It includes a command line editor.

Bash (*Bourne again shell*) came from the FSF (Free Software Foundation). It combines the best of the C-shell and the Korn-shell. It can be configured in many different ways and was the standard Linux shell from the beginning.

Although it has lot of characteristics in common with the C-shell, it is also similar to the Bourne shell and the Korn shell, and its programming syntax can be compatible with them both. In addition, it offers its own particular characteristics.

The shell is the interactive part of the system. It allows you to use the system more or less efficiently according to the shell you use. It is very important, therefore, to understand how to execute commands with a shell. In this book we will limit ourselves to **bash**. It must be remembered, however, that many of the syntax rules are incompatible with the C-shell and that there is a certain backwards compatibility with the Bourne shell.

(kernel version 2.0 à 2.2)

Chapter 7

As the shell you work with is your intermediary with the system, it is important that you know it well. Moreover, in view of the vast possibilities it offers, the better you know your shell, the easier it will be for you to optimize its environment.

B. Entering commands

You can enter a command as soon as the shell allows you to. The shell indicates that it is ready to receive a command by displaying a prompt in the form of a dollar sign ($):

```
$ pwd
/home/ftp
$
```

However, even if the prompt has not been displayed, you can still type in characters, which will be memorized for display on the screen when the prompt re-appears. When you have entered the command line, confirm it by pressing the Enter key.

If the command line contains an error, you can edit it in various ways. However, you must specify the editor mode that **bash** must use. You can choose either **vi** or **emacs** mode. Our preference is the **vi** mode (command line editing will be outlined in this chapter and then covered more fully in chapter 9, which deals specifically with the **vi** editor).

C. Editing a command

Use the **set** command to specify the editor mode, as in the following example, where **vi** is selected:

```
$ set -o vi
```

Only basic command editing functions will be covered here. Other functions are available and will be presented in chapter 9.

To correct a command line go into **command** mode by pressing the [Esc] key. In this mode, you can input commands from the keyboard.

Here are a few examples of commands which allow you to move the cursor (you can also use the arrow keys):

      h previous character
      l next character
      ^ start of the line
      $ end of the line
      w start of next word
      b start of previous word
      fc move right to the next "c" character on the current line

Each of these commands (except for ^ and $) can be prefixed by a number. For example, **3w** will move the cursor to the start of the third word to the right.

It is important to know these few basic commands as many others are derived from them.

For instance, prefixing these commands with a **d** character changes them into delete commands. Similarly, preceding them with a **y** character turns them into copy commands and prefixing a **c** character turns them into change (replace) commands.

(kernel version 2.0 à 2.2)

For example, if you enter **5dl** you will delete the 5 characters to the right starting from the position of the cursor: entering **3yb** will copy the three words to the left of the word on which the cursor is positioned.

It must be noted that deleted characters are stored temporarily in a buffer in the same way as those copied using **y**-prefixed commands.

You can paste the contents of this buffer where you like in the line using the **p** or the **P** command. The **p** command inserts to the right of the cursor, whereas **P** inserts to the left.

Change commands delete specified characters and take you into input mode.

Here are some other editing commands which have the same effect as some of those discussed above, but which are often quicker to use:

- **x** deletes the character under the cursor.
- **X** deletes the character to the right of the cursor.
- **rc** replaces the character under the cursor with the character "c".
- **D** deletes all the characters to the end of the line
- **yy** copies the current line
- **dd** deletes the current line

Once the corrections have been made, go back into input mode using one of the following keys:

- **i** goes into input mode; the characters are inserted before the cursor
- **I** goes into input mode; the characters are inserted at the beginning of the current line
- **a** goes into input mode; the characters are inserted after the cursor

> **A** goes into input mode; the characters are inserted after the end of the current line

There are other commands that make command editing easier. A sound approach to working with Linux is always to do what you want with a minimum of effort, and the bash is very good at helping you to do this. For example to enter a command or a file name, type enough letters so that it can be identified without ambiguity, and the bash will input the rest for you. Two commands allow you to use this facility in **vi** mode:

\   using this command in **vi** after entering the first part of the word, produces one of the following results:

① If there is a shell built-in command, an alias, a function, a file or a directory that can be identified without ambiguity, then the shell completes the name of the item concerned and then allows you to carry on entering the command line as necessary. It must be noted that command names, aliases and functions have priority over file names. If the item is recognized as a directory, the name will be followed by a slash (/). In certain cases, the shell will limit its search as follows:
− if the character string is preceded by a $ character, the shell will display only variable names beginning with the character string concerned.
− if the character string is preceded by a ~ character, the shell will attempt to form a username
− if the character string is preceded by a @ character, the shell will search for the name of a machine.

(kernel version 2.0 à 2.2)

② If the shell finds nothing beginning with the character string entered, it emits a beep.

③ If there is ambiguity between several items (all beginning with the character string entered) the shell will choose that item name which has the largest common root.

* The * command works in the same way as /, except that if there is any ambiguity, rather than choosing the item with the largest common root, all the possibilities will be displayed on the line.

The = command is used for information purposes and displays all the commands, aliases, functions, files and directories beginning with the character string preceding it. It does not act on the command line.

D. Aliases

An alias is an abbreviation or alternative name which is used instead of a command or a group of words. Alliases allow you to reduce typing of commonly used commands. They also allow you to define new default options. You can define an alias in a command line (it will be recognized only until the end of the session). Alternatively, you can define your aliases in a personal initialization file, which allows you to use them from one session to the next.

1. Defining an alias

An alias is defined as follows:

```
alias NAME=TEXT
```

The name of an alias must never begin with a special character, but it can include letters and/or digits.

To avoid any ambiguity, it is strongly advisable to use apostrophes when defining an alias:

```
alias NAME='TEXT'
```

An alias is substituted by its definition before all other substitutions are made on the command line. Moreover, alias substitutions are made only if the alias is the first word on the command line.

```
$ alias ll='ls -l'
$ ll /home/ftp
total 8
dr-xr-xr-x   2 root     root         1024 Jan  9 21:51 pub/
r-xr-xr-x    2 root     root         1024 Aug 14 14:37 dev/
dr-xr-xr-x   2 root     root         1024 Aug 13 16:21 etc/
drwxrwxrwt   4 root     root         1024 Jan 10 13:14 incoming/
dr-xr-xr-x   2 root     root         1024 Nov 17  1993 lib/
dr-xr-xr-x   2 root     root         1024 Jan  9 21:51 pub/
dr-xr-xr-x   3 root     root         1024 Sep 23 21:22 usr/
-rw-r--r--   1 root     root          312 Aug  1  1994 welcome.msg
```

To enable a further substitution to be made in an adjacent string, the preceding substitution must end with a space:

```
$ alias l='ls -l'
$ alias b='/home/ftp'
$ l b
/bin/ls: b: No such file or directory
```

(kernel version 2.0 à 2.2)

Chapter 7

```
$ alias l='ls -l '
$ alias b='/home/ftp'
$ l b
total 8
dr-xr-xr-x   2 root     root         1024 Dec  3  1993 bin/
dr-xr-xr-x   2 root     root         1024 Aug 14 14:37 dev/
dr-xr-xr-x   2 root     root         1024 Aug 13 16:21 etc/
drwxrwx-wt   4 root     root         1024 Jan 10 13:14
incoming/
dr-xr-xr-x   2 root     root         1024 Nov 17  1993 lib/
dr-xr-xr-x   2 root     root         1024 Jan  9 21:51 pub/
dr-xr-xr-x   3 root     root         1024 Sep 23 21:22 usr/
-rw-r--r--   1 root     root          312 Aug  1  1994 welcome.msg
```

Aliases are not normally exported. They are therefore not normally available in shell scripts, unless their definition is included in a file and the **ENV** variable is initialized with the name of this file.

However, it is preferable to export using functions instead of aliases. As functions are more in the field of shell programming they are beyond the scope of this book.

2. Listing current aliases

The **alias** command without parameters lists existing aliases, for example:

```
$ alias
alias clean='rm -f *%'
alias cp='cp -i'
alias d='dir'
alias dir='/bin/ls $LS_OPTIONS --format=vertical'
alias l='less'
alias ll='ls -l'
alias lock='xlock -nice 0 -mode blank &'
alias ls='/bin/ls $LS_OPTIONS'
alias mv='mv -i'
alias rm='rm -i'
alias screen='xlock -nolock -nice 0 -mode blank &'
alias up='cd ..'
alias v='vdir'
alias vdir='/bin/ls $LS_OPTIONS --format=long' 3.
```

3. Deleting an alias

To delete an alias use the **unalias** command followed by the name(s) of the alias(es) you wish to delete:

```
$ unalias ll l
```

E. History and command substitutions

The command *history* mechanism appeared with the *C-shell* and was incorporated in later shells such as the *Korn shell*, the *bash* and the *tcsh*. It keeps a certain number of previously-executed commands in memory so that you can re-use them without having to re-type them in full. This facility, combined with the other command-line editing features and the various shell parameters available, provides you with more power and productivity than you would obtain from a graphical interface (first however, you must take the time to master the environment configuration techniques).

By default, the 500 last commands you executed are stored in the **$HOME/.bash_history** file ($HOME invokes the HOME environment variable which contains the name of your HOME directory). When you open a session the shell loads the contents of the history file into memory. Each session keeps its own list of commands and writes them to the history file at the end of the session.

Three variables allow you to modify these parameters:

HISTFILE can be used to indicate another name for the history file.

HISTFILESIZE defines the number of commands that can be stored in the history file (500 by default).

(kernel version 2.0 à 2.2)

HISTSIZE defines the number of commands that can be contained in the command list of each session (500 by default).

The complete list of the last 500 (or however many commands are indicated in the HISTSIZE variable), commands can be displayed using the shell built-in **history** command. However, this command is much less flexible to use than **fc**. This shell built-in command which originated with the Korn shell allows you not only to display the history list, but also to re-execute the commands after modifying them as required. This command is described below.

1. Displaying the command history

The **fc** command is used for working with the command history list. To display this list use the **-l** option.

By default, **fc -l** displays the last 16 commands along with their command numbers:

```
$ fc -l
585      ls
586      less *man
587      make man
588      make
589      less README
590      configure
591      make
592      ls
593      make -n install
594      less *.nro
595      su
596      man -t >|f1
597      man -t less>|f1
598      gv f1
599      biff
600      lock
601      fc -l
```

If you specify the **-n** option, the command numbers do not appear.

In the case of one argument:
- if the argument is an (unsigned) number, **fc -l** displays the latest commands starting with the command having the number specified. If the number is preceded by a dash (-), the last *number* of commands will be displayed (example: **fc -l -5** displays the last 5 commands).
- if the argument is a character string, **fc -l** displays the last commands, starting with the most recent command to begin with the character string concerned.

```
$ fc -l 592
592        ls
593        make -n install
594        less *.nro
595        su
596        man -t >|f1
597        man -t less>|f1
598        gv f1
599        biff
600        lock
601        fc -l
602        fc -l 592
$ fc -l ma
597        man -t less>|f1
598        gv f1
599        biff
600        lock
601        fc -l
602        fc -l 592
603        fc -l ma
```

In the case of two arguments:

The first argument specifies the start of the command history display and the second argument specifies the end of the command history display.

(kernel version 2.0 à 2.2)

These arguments can be numbers, character strings or a combination of the two. In addition, numerical argument(s) can be absolute values, in which case they correspond to command numbers, or they can be relative values. In the case of character strings, the bash always starts with the most recent command beginning with the characters concerned. Here are a few examples:

```
$ fc -l
491       man bash
492       alias
493       type history
494       fc -l
495       cat f1
496       df
497       cd /var/account/
498       lm
499       su -
500       exit
501       cd cours/shell/
502       ksh
503       fc -l
504       fc -l -10 lm
505       fc -l 500
506      *fc -l
507       lm
$ fc -l 497 500
497       cd /var/account/
498       lm
499       su -
500       exit
$ fc -l 497 ex
497       cd /var/account/
498       lm
499       su -
500       exit
$ fc -l -14 ex
497       cd /var/account/
498       lm
499       su -
500       exit
$ fc -l cd ex
501       cd cours/shell/
500       exit
```

The main use of the command history is to find a command, to modify it (if necessary) and to execute it. This sequence will now be described.

2. Recalling and editing a command

You can recall one or more commands in three different ways; one unique to the bash and using the shell built-in **fc** command, and the other two specific to the command-line editing mode. We will concentrate on the **fc** command as this can be used whatever editing mode you choose.

First, use **fc -l** (see above) to list the numbers of the commands you wish to recall, or to find out which characters they start with.

As soon as you know the sequence number of a command, you can recall it for execution, either directly or after modification.

> If no command number is indicated to **fc**, only the last command will be recalled.

Using **fc** without any option will recall the commands specified by the command arguments so that you can edit them. The default editor is **vi**. If you prefer, you can specify a different editor:

1. You can use the **-e** option followed by the name of the editor required. This can be any editor present on your system, even editors such as **xedit**, **textedit** or **nedit**, which run on X11. So that you do not have to specify the editor every time you want to use it, **fc** works with two system variables when it is invoked without the **-e** option (system variables are discussed in sections F and G of this chapter (**set** command)).

(kernel version 2.0 à 2.2)

2. The first variable that **fc** uses is FCEDIT which, if defined, must contain the path to the required editor. If this variable is not defined, **fc** uses the editor path specified in the EDITOR variable.

We remind you that if the **-e** option is not used and neither FCEDIT nor EDITOR is defined, then **vi** will be the editor used by default.

In all cases, the command will be executed when the user leaves the editor.

It is also possible to re-execute a command without using the editor. To do this, use **fc -e -**. The minus sign following the **-e** option indicates that the editor must not be invoked.

As mentioned previously, you can edit and re-execute several commands. To do this, you must specify two numbers or character strings, as when displaying commands, and all the commands included between these two indicators will be recalled.

Warning: when you recall several commands they will be executed after you have finished editing. This can be dangerous as it is not always easy to master the action produced by a sequence of commands, especially when the sequence is relatively long.

Instead of doing this, it is advisable to use the following method:
− redirect the output of the **fc -ln n1 n2** (into a **cmd** file for example, cf. Chapter 8). The **-n** option is used here to ensure that command numbers do not appear in the file so that they do not cause problems on execution,
− edit the file: **vi cmd**
− execute the file using the **source cmd** command.

By this means, you keep control of each step, rather than running them automatically, one after the other.

```
$ fc -ln >cmd
$ vi cmd
$ source cmd
uid=504(system) gid=100(users) groups=100(users)
 0 (wheel)
system    ttyp0      Feb 10 09:12 (:0.0)
system    ttyp1      Feb 15 10:35 (:0.0)
system    ttyp3      Feb 15 09:46 (arthur.dorset.)
system    ttyp4      Feb 15 11:25 (:0.0)
```

3. Immediate substitution

Suppose that you wish to execute the following command:
```
ls /usr/local/lib
```

and the previous command was:
```
ls /usr/local/bin
```

As these commands are very similar, it would be useful to have a way to avoid entering the whole command. This is possible using the **-s** option of the **fc** command which allows you to substitute a character string in a previous command. Here is the syntax:
```
fc -s OLD=NEW [COMMAND]
```

fc uses the command identified by its number, its relative position or its initial characters. If COMMAND is not specified, **fc** uses the last command executed.

```
$ ls -l /usr/local/etc
total 9
-rw-r--r--   1 root    root       9040 Feb 11 20:36
xferstats.cfg
$ fc -s etc=sbin
ls -l /usr/local/sbin
total 268
-rwxr--r--   1 root    root        402 Feb  7 18:32 auth.
trim
-rwxr-xr-x   1 root    bin        6428 Feb  5 21:33 fail
log
-rwx------   1 root    sys       74054 Feb  4 11:54 lsof
-r-xr-xr-x   1 root    bin       10324 Feb 14 20:44
newsyslog
-rwx------   1 root    root       3868 Nov  1  1997
sulog.trim
-r-xr-x---   1 bin     wheel    173174 Feb 18  1998
tcpdump
```

4. Using C-shell type history commands

If you are accustomed to using the C-shell you will be pleased to learn that the *bash* also offers the command recall mechanism used by *C-shell*.

In spite of the fact that this mechanism offers fewer possibilities than the **fc** command, it is still very convenient to use in certain situations.

Here are the C-shell recall commands that you can use:

!! re-execute the last command

!n re-execute the command number n

!-n re-execute the nth last command (current command -n)

!string re-execute the latest command beginning with the indicated character string

!?string re-execute the latest command containing the indicated character string

Although these commands have a slightly different approach, they will not be covered in more detail here as they are largely redundant with command editing techniques. Because of this, these commands are used less and less. We believe it is preferable to spend time mastering editor mode techniques rather than learning a mechanism that is present mainly to provide compatibility with the *C-shell*.

F. Environment variables

This section provides a brief description of variables, notably of the environment variables.

A variable is a memory location, which has been given a name so that you can work with it more conveniently. A variable is a container.

As with Unix, Linux supports two types of variable:
— environment variables, created and maintained by the shell
— user variables, created and maintained by each user

Environment variables will be covered here.

By convention, and it is only a convention, environment variable names are composed exclusively of upper-case letters and digits; lower-case letters are reserved for the names of user variables.

The role of environment variables is to make certain information on the current session available to the shell and the system. This information is dynamic and must therefore be kept up-to-date.

(kernel version 2.0 à 2.2)

Environment variables include the following:

- **USER** contains your username. It is redundant with the LOGNAME variable
- **HOME** contains the home directory path
- **PWD** contains the name of the current working directory
- **OLDPWD** contains the name of the directory you were in last.
- **SHELL** contains the location of your shell. This variable is common to all Bourne shells. **bash** also uses the BASH variable.
- **PS1** defines the prompt. To customize the prompt see below.
- **PS2** defines the secondary prompt string. This prompt will appear when you validate a command line and the shell realizes that the command is syntactically incomplete: for example, if you enter a single apostrophe where the shell expects two, or if the line finishes with a \ character (the use of this character is described below).
- **PS3 and PS4** are other prompts which are used less frequently and more specifically for shell programming.

Environment variable contents can be displayed using the **echo** or the **set** command. These two commands will be covered in the next section (Shell built-in commands).

Reminder: Environment variables are maintained by the shell and many of them must never be modified directly by users, even though it is possible to do so. The danger is not necessarily very great in all cases, but it can alter how the shell works, as we will see in the case of the **cd** command, which uses the HOME, PWD and OLDPWD variables.

G. Shell built-in commands

Shell built-in commands are commands that are integrated with the shell. This means that they are not independent binary files (in contrast to shell-external commands such as **ls**, **cat**, **cut** ...).

Another difference comes from the fact that shell built-in commands are executed inside the shell, whereas shell-external commands necessitate the creation of processes (cf Chapter 14, section E, Process Management).

The objective here is not to present the whole set of commands by menu, for two reasons:
- some shell built-in commands are of limited interest to most users
- other shell built-in commands are more for use in scripts, although it is quite possible to use them in a command line (shell scripts are system programs, which are outside the scope of this book).

echo

The **echo** command displays on the standard output, the text that was passed as an argument followed by a new line. In the absence of an argument, only the new line will be output.

This command has the following options:
- **-e** enables the interpretation of escape sequences
- **-n** inhibits the final new line.

Escape sequences allow the display of characters or actions that are not normally available using keys on the keyboard. They are introduced by the \ character.

(kernel version 2.0 à 2.2)

Chapter 7

\a   to emit a beep (bell)
\b   backspace: if it appears at the end of the character string it must be used with the **-n** option or else it will be automatically placed after the new line and will therefore have no effect.
\c   inhibits the final new line (equivalent to **-n**)
\f   form feed (according to the type of terminal this may be interpreted as one or several new lines or else by the clearing of the screen).
\n   new line
\r   carriage return
\t   horizontal tab
\v   vertical tab
\nnn   the character for which the ASCII code is nnn (1 to 3 octal digits).
****   the \ character.

To display the contents of a variable, prefix the variable name with the $ character.

```
$ echo display text
display text
$ variable="variable contents"
$ echo $variable
variable contents
```

set

This is an essential shell command. It has a number of uses, one of the main ones being to activate and deactivate shell options. Shell options allow you to adapt the functioning of the shell to suit your needs. They are therefore important when you configure your user's environment.

To activate a shell option, use the following syntax:

```
set -o option
```

Similarly, to deactivate a shell option use the following syntax

```
set +o option
```

Here are some of the more useful shell options:

allexport the variables defined after setting this option will be automatically exported.

bgnice background processes are assigned a higher nice factor (lower priority) and will therefore execute more slowly.

emacs the **emacs** editor mode will be used

vi the **vi** editor mode will be used

histexpand activates the C-shell command recall mechanism

ignoreeof When this option is set the Ctrl D shortcut key will not disconnect you. This can avoid problems as this shortcut key is used to terminate the input of data to a filter.

monitor activates job control

noclobber Simple redirection to an existing file is not allowed. To do this you must use ">|" (cf. Chapter 8, section C.1, Redirecting output).

noglob inhibits the wildcard meanings of * and ? characters

nohash inhibits the memorization of command paths. Activating this option should be avoided for performance reasons.

notify to inform you as soon as a background task finishes, rather than awaiting the next prompt.

xtrace displays commands as they will be executed, after complete parsing of the command line

(kernel version 2.0 à 2.2)

The **set -o** command lists all options along with their states:

```
$ set -o
braceexpand         on
noclobber           on
ignoreeof           on
interactive-comments    on
posix               off
emacs               on
vi                  off
allexport           off
rrexit              off
histexpand          on
monitor             on
noexec              off
noglob              off
nohash              off
notify              off
nounset             off
physical            off
privileged          off
verbose             off
xtrace              off
```

Furthermore, the **set** command without options or arguments displays the variables of the current shell along with their values.

```
$ set
CDPATH
DISPLAY
ENV
FCEDIT
FPATH
HISTFILE=.hist
HOME=/home/toto
HOSTNAME=merlin.dorset.uk
IFS=

KSH_VERSION='@(#)PD KSH v5.2.8 96/08/19'
LESS=-MM
LESSOPEN='|lesspipe.sh %s'
LOGNAME=toto
...
...
```

```
OLDPWD=/home/ftp/pub
OPENWINHOME=/usr/openwin
OPTIND=1
PATH=/bin:/usr/bin:/usr/X11/bin:/usr/local/bin:/
usr/openwin/bn
PPID=330
PS1='! $ '
PS2=' '
PS3='#? '
PS4='+ '
PWD=/home/ftp
RANDOM=12119
SECOND
SECONDS=26524
SHELL=/usr/local/bin/ksh
TERM=vt100
TMOUT=0
USER=toto
VISUAL
_=set
ignoreeof=10
```

pwd

This command displays the current working directory, whose name is stored in the PWD variable.

```
$ pwd
/home/ftp
$ echo $PWD
/home/ftp
```

cd

This command allows you to change your working directory. The new working directory is passed as an argument to this command.

```
$ pwd
/usr
$ cd /home/ftp
$ pwd
/home/ftp
```

The PWD variable is updated as soon as its contents have been transferred to OLDPWD.

```
$ echo $OLDPWD
/home/ftp
$ echo $PWD
/home/toto
```

cd allows you to return to the previous working directory, the name of which is contained in OLDPWD.

```
$ pwd
/home/ftp
$ cd /usr/local
$ pwd
/usr/local
$ cd -
/home/ftp
$ pwd
/home/ftp
```

When returning to the previous working directory, the **cd** command uses the OLDPWD contents as its reference. The following example demonstrates this mechanism:

```
$ pwd
/home/toto
$ echo $OLDPWD
/home/ftp
$ OLDPWD=/bin
$ cd -
/bin
```

Used without an argument, **cd** allows you to return to your home directory, contained in the HOME variable (the command **cd ~** has the same effect).

```
$ logname
system
$ pwd
/home/ftp
$ cd
$ pwd
/home/system
```

Here again, the shell uses an environment variable as its reference, in this case the HOME variable which is initialized at the start of the session. It contains the path of the home directory. It is easy to modify this for the current session:

```
$ cd /bin
$ pwd
/bin
$ echo $HOME
/home/system
$ cd
$ pwd
/home/system
$ HOME=/tmp
$ cd
$ pwd
/tmp
```

dirs, pushd, popd

The **cd** command provides a first approach to moving around in the file hierarchy by allowing you to commute between current and previous working directories. We will now examine a more complete mechanism using the stack concept.

The paths for commands are memorized automatically by the shell, if you want the shell. However, if you want the shell to memorize a directory you must specifically request it. You can do this by calling the **pushd** command followed by the name of the directory. This action results in the following steps being carried out:
— add the current directory to the list of memorized directories
— change the current working directory to that indicated
— add this new working directory to the list of memorized directories
— display the list of memorized directories

```
$ pwd
/bin
$ pushd /etc
/etc /bin
$ pwd
/etc
$ pushd /sbin
/sbin /etc /bin
$ pwd
/sbin
$ pushd /tmp
/tmp /sbin /etc /bin
$ pwd
/tmp
```

Use the **dirs** command to display the contents of the list of memorized directories:

```
$ dirs
~ /sbin /etc /bin
$ dirs -l
/home/system /sbin /etc /bin
```

The ~ character represents the home directory. Using the command with the **-l** option replaces the ~ character with the actual name of the home directory. This can be useful if the contents of the list are stored in a file, to be used later by another user for whom ~ may have a different meaning.

Once the list has been constructed, you can go to one of the directories contained in it using the **pushd** command.

pushd without arguments allows you to switch between the top two directories in the list:

```
$ dirs
/tmp /sbin /etc /bin
$ pushd
/sbin /tmp /etc /bin
$ pwd
/sbin
$ pushd
/tmp /sbin /etc /bin
$ pwd
/tmp
```

A similar rotation can be made between the directory at the top of the list (which is always the current working directory) and the **n**th directory in the list. Use **-n** to indicate the **n**th element from the bottom (right) of the list, or **+n** to indicate the **n**th element from the top (left) of the list. It must be noted that you start counting from 0 (zero) and that **pushd +0** keeps you in the same directory:

```
$ dirs
/etc /sbin /tmp /bin
$ pushd +0
/etc /sbin /tmp /bin
$ pushd +3
/bin /etc /sbin /tmp
$ pwd
/bin
$ pushd -2
/etc /sbin /tmp /bin
$ pwd
/etc
```

In certain circumstances, you may wish to delete elements in the list. This can be done using the **popd** command. Used without arguments this command deletes the current working directory from the list with the result that the next directory in the list becomes the current working directory:

```
$ dirs
/etc /sbin /tmp /bin
$ pwd
/etc
$ popd
/sbin /tmp /bin
$ pwd
/sbin
```

If you want to delete another directory in the list, select it using the same convention as for **pushd**:

> **-n** to delete the **n**th element from the bottom (right) of the list
>
> **+n** to delete the **n**th element from the top (left) of the list

(kernel version 2.0 à 2.2)

+0 equivalent to **popd** without an argument

```
$ dirs
/var /sbin /tmp /bin
$ popd -1
/var /sbin /bin
$ popd +2
/var /sbin
$ popd +0
/sbin
$ pwd
/sbin
```

hash

As long as the **nohash** option is not set, each time the shell executes a command, it looks for it in the set of directories contained in the PATH variable. Once the shell has found the command, it memorizes its path so as to optimize performance by not having to search for it in future.

The **hash** command allows you to manage this hash table:
– by displaying its contents
– by adding new entries
– by deleting its contents

The first of these actions is carried out using the **hash** command without options or arguments. It displays the command names for which the paths have been memorized by the shell, along with the number of times each of these commands has been executed.

To make the shell remember a new command path, you need only execute the **hash** command with the name of the command as an argument.

To delete the contents of the hash list, use the **hash** command with the **-r** (remove) option.

```
$ hash
hits    command
   1    /usr/bin/biff
   1    /usr/bin/mesg
   6    /usr/bin/man
   1    /usr/local/bin/ksh
   4    /bin/more
   2    /bin/id
   2    /bin/who
   4    /usr/bin/vi
   1    /bin/su
$ hash cat
$ hash mail
$ hash
hits    command
   0    /bin/cat
   0    /bin/mail
   1    /usr/bin/biff
   1    /usr/bin/mesg
   7    /usr/bin/man
   1    /usr/bin/passwd
   1    /usr/local/bin/ksh
   4    /bin/more
   2    /bin/id
   2    /bin/who
   4    /usr/bin/vi
   1    /bin/su
$ hash -r
$ hash
No commands in hash table.
```

Warning: The **hash -r cmd** command will not delete a **cmd** entry in the table. It will empty the table and then add the **cmd** command.

command

In most cases, alias names correspond to shell-external command names in such a way as to specify a default option. For example, **rm** is often used as an alias for **rm -i**. However, it may be necessary, and even essential to bypass an alias expansion. For this, use the **command** command followed by the command as it should be entered.

(kernel version 2.0 à 2.2)

```
$ alias rm
alias rm='rm -i'
$ rm f1
rm: remove 'f1'? n
$ command rm f1
$ ls f1
/bin/ls: f1: No such file or directory
```

All that **command** does is to specify the execution of shell built-in commands, or the execution of shell-external commands which, must be sought directly using the PATH variable without looking for an alias. Consequently, any name specified which corresponds neither to a shell built-in command, nor to a shell-external command present in the PATH, will result in an error message:

```
$ alias up
alias up='cd ..'
$ command up
bash: up: command not found
```

You might be wondering how you can find out if a word corresponds to a command, an alias, a function or nothing that the shell can understand. This information can be obtained using the **type** command.

type

This very useful command tells you what the shell considers an item to be:

```
$ type cat rm cd if thing
cat is /bin/cat
rm is aliased to 'rm -i'cd is a shell builtin
if is a shell keyword
type: thing: not found
```

In the above example, five item names were passed for scrutiny by the **type** command: a shell-external command, an alias, a shell built-in command, a keyword and an unknown item.

You can also ask the **type** command to return only the type of the items passed using the **-type** option:

```
$ type -type cat rm cd if thing
file
alias
builtin
keyword
```

It must be noted that **-type** does not distinguish between a file and a directory:

```
$ ls -ld mbox tmp
-rw-------   1 system   users     11592 Feb 14 17:35 mbox
drwxr-xr-x   2 system   users      1024 Feb 11 22:05 tmp/
$ type -type mbox tmp
file
file
```

Also, instead of the type of the items, you can request only their paths using the **path** option:

```
$type -path cat rm cd if thing
/bin/cat
```

As for the **-type** option, any item not concerned by this option is simply ignored.

```
$ type rm cd
rm is aliased to 'rm -i'
cd is a shell builtin
$ type -path rm cd
$ which rm cd
/bin/rm
which: no cd in   (/bin:/usr/bin:/usr/X11R6/bin:/usr
/local/bin:
/usr/openwin/bin:/home/system/bin:/usr/local/pgsql/
bin:.:/usr/
local/samba/bin:)
```

(kernel version 2.0 à 2.2)

It must be noted that **type -path** is equivalent to the shell-external **which** command, except that the latter searches for the items passed as arguments only in the PATH directories. The **which** command does not attempt to find out whether there may be a shell built-in command, an alias or a function with the same name. In contrast, **type -path** returns nothing if an argument is a shell built-in command, an alias or a function, because of the shell internal priority. This will be covered in the "Parsing the command line" section.

Other shell built-in commands are dealt with in other sections of this book, as we believe they are better described in their respective contexts rather than in this list.

H. Meta-characters and special characters

A meta-character is a sort of "wildcard" that replaces one or several characters. There are four of them:

- ? replaces any character
- * replaces a set of 0 to n characters of any type
- [character list] replaces any character that appears in the list between the square brackets
- [!character list] replaces any character except those appearing in the list between the square brackets

In contrast to square brackets which replace one character at a time, braces {} can be used to indicate alternative character strings:

```
ls -1 *.{new,exo,?a}
bin.aa.new
bin.ab.new
bin.ac.new
bin.ad.new
bin.ae.new
bin.af.new
bin.ba.ba
bin.bc.new
bin.ca.ca
bin.da.da
cut.exo
egrep.exo
expand.exo
grep.exo
sort.exo
sort2.exo
tr.exo
uniq.exo
```

It must be noted that you can use meta-characters inside braces.

Special characters, by default, do not represent themselves but have a special meaning for the shell. There are five of them:

- ' inhibits the interpretation of meta-characters or special characters (appearing between two of these apostrophes)

- " inhibits the interpretation of meta-characters or special characters and prevent the special interpretation of the apostrophe (appearing between two of these quotation marks)

- ` executes a command (appearing between two of these backquotes) as if it appeared on a line by itself

(kernel version 2.0 à 2.2)

\ inhibits the interpretation of the special character appearing immediately after it. It must be noted that the bash, in common with the Korn-shell, offers a more flexible syntax: $(cmd).

$ allows you to use the contents of a variable (when prefixed to the variable name)

Meta-characters and special characters allow you to create models. For example, if you want to list all the files in a directory, instead of entering a print command for each file you can use the * character.

Here are a few examples of the use of meta-characters and special characters:

```
$ ls -1 *[0-9]
diff1
diff2
f1
f2
job1
job2
job3
job4
join1
join2
paste.exo1
paste.exo2
sort1
sort2
$ ls -1 [!a-r]*[!0-9]
save.log
session*
sort.exo
sort2.exo
tr.exo
uniq.exo
vi.sub
$ echo login name : $USER
login name : system
$ echo login name : `logname`
login name : system
$ echo login name : $(logname)
login name : system
$ echo "login name : $USER"
login name : system
$ echo 'login name : $USER'
login name : $USER
```

I. Parsing the command line

We have already seen that the shell works with the following items:
- aliases
- special characters and meta-characters
- shell built-in commands

In addition, as we will see, it is possible to create functions.

In total, with shell-external commands (independent of the shell) a command line can contain up to five component types.

Understanding how the shell parses a command line is essential. Here is an example of a command line:
```
ll $PRE*.c
```

We remind you that the **ll** (double-ell) here is the alias of the **ls -l** command.

The PRE variable contains the **mprog_** string; in the example this is used to prefix the filenames of a development project. The output could include the following files:
```
mprog_main.c
mprog_fonc.c
mprog_res.c
```

In general the shell goes through the following sequence:
1) Display the $ prompt
2) Read the line on the standard input
   (by default the keyboard)
3) Parse the line
   - 3.1 Split-up the command line into its component parts
   - 3.2 Substitute any aliases then return to 3.1

(kernel version 2.0 à 2.2)

- 3.3 Parse "protection" characters:', ", \
  Substitute values for variable names prefixed by a $
- 3.4 Substitute any commands appearing between backquotes (')
- 3.5 Substitute Meta-characters: expand file names
- 3.6 Handle any re-directions
- 3.7 Execute the shell-built-in command

  or

  3.8 Create a sub-process (in the case of a shell external command)

Here is the parsing sequence for the above command:

ll $PRE*.c

∨

ls -l $PRE*.c

∨

ls -l mprog_*.c

∨

ls -l mprog_main.c mprog_fonc.c mprog_res.c

∨

Displays the result.

J. Initializing the environment

Environment configuration is not dealt with in a separate chapter as it depends heavily on the user's login shell. In fact, initialization is done using a number of configuration files, for which the names and functions vary from one shell to another.

We will limit ourselves here to environment configuration carried out with **bash**.

Several files are used for this configuration. One of these, **/etc/profile**, is common to all users and is read at the start of each session. **bash** uses this file to set up a minimal configuration common to all users. Then, **bash** searches for the customized configuration file of each user, in their respective home directories. Several names are possible for this file: the shell will search first for **.bash_profile**, then for **.bash_login**, if the first file is not found, and then for **.profile**, if **.bash_login** is also absent.

In this file, you can include whatever you like to customize the prompt, file-creation-mode masks.... In general, however, this file must contain very little. As it is read only when the user logs in, it will not be consulted by shells started from the command line. Nor will it be consulted by shells associated with **xterm** graphical windows, unless xterm is called using the **-ls** option (*login shell*).

However, these non-login shells can be configured using the **.bashrc** file (the **rc** suffix stands for **run command**). It is generally this file that contains the set of configuration commands that can be used by all the user's shells. The reading of this file is requested in the **.bash_profile** file as follows:

```
source .bashrc
```

In addition, so that scripts can use the definitions contained in this file (such as aliases, functions and various variables) it is advisable to initialize the **ENV** variable with the name of this file and to export it:

```
export ENV=.bashrc
```

A final functionality that can be useful is the customization of the prompt.

(kernel version 2.0 à 2.2)

K. Customizing the prompt

In common with the *Bourne-shell* and the *Korn-shell*, the default prompt for *bash* is the $ character for all users, except *root* for whom the prompt by default is the # character.

As the prompt is associated with the PS1 environment variable, a user can always change it, for example, to give the impression of working with the C-shell or even of being the system administrator.

```
$ PS1="% "
% PS1="# "
#
```

Far from being just a static value, the prompt can contain such variable values as the current working directory, the name of the user and the date. In the example below, the PS1 variable is defined so that the prompt displays the command number, the user name, the machine name and the current working directory.

```
$ PS1="[\#]-\u(\h)\w:"
[62]-system(merlin)~: cd /tmp
[63]-system(merlin)/tmp:
```

The following sequences can be used to customize your prompt:

\d current date

\h name of the machine

\n new line

\s name of the shell

\t current time in hh:mm:ss format

\u user name

\w current working directory

\# command number from login

\! command history number

\$ default prompt: # for root, $ otherwise

\nnn character for which the ASCII code is 1 to 3 octal digits

\\ back-slash

Chapter 8

Redirecting inputs and outputs

- A. **Structure of a command** 98
- B. **Concept of standard streams** 100
- C. **Redirecting standard streams** 101
   1. Redirecting output 101
   2. Adding items to the end of a file 102
   3. Redirecting input 102
   4. Duplicating streams 103
   5. Opening a new stream 104
- D. **Connecting commands using pipes** 106

Using Linux

As we have seen, a Unix or Linux command is a building block that does one thing, but does it well. It is left to the user to combine these blocks together to respond to a particular need.

In this chapter we will look at techniques that allow you to fit commands together. Everything presented in this chapter assumes you are using a *Bourne-shell*, a *Korn-shell* or *bash* and will be valid for all of these shells unless specifically stated otherwise.

There are two basic ways of combining commands together: by redirecting inputs and outputs, and by pipes. However, before discussing these techniques, we will look at the general command structure.

A. Structure of a command

The original objective of Unix was to provide an operating system to handle files. The original specification also stipulated that the system was not to deal with structured files but that each file was to be considered simply as a stream of bytes like any other stream of bytes. Consequently, Unix was equipped with a large number of utilities to treat byte streams, wherever they may come from: files, keyboards or other input peripherals.

These commands accept bytes from input streams, process them and produce output streams. When an error occurs it appears on what is called an error stream. In summary, these commands have three streams:
– an input stream, number 0
– an output stream, number 1
– an error stream, number 2

```
input_stream →name[options] →output_stream
                     ↓
              error_stream
```

Commands that conform to this model are called **filters**, because input bytes are processed to produce output bytes. A typical example of a filter is the **grep** command, which accepts input (text) lines and outputs only those text lines that contain a specified character string (**grep** will be covered in greater detail later). However, the concept of a filter is much wider than this; it applies to all com*/mands that work with both input and output streams. Later we will see how simple it is to combine these filters together.

However, all commands do not correspond to this model. Some commands do not have an input stream, but work only with arguments. An example of this type of command is **ls**: it allows you to view, for example, the contents of a directory whose name is passed as an argument, or by default, those of the current working directory.

Other commands work with an input stream but produce results according to an argument or a default value. A typical example of this is the **lpr** command, which prints all byte streams coming from the keyboard, or from a file.

As we have seen, when a command works with an input and an output stream, by default these are the keyboard and the screen respectively. You can, however, specify these streams in other ways, but before we examine them, we will look more closely at the concept of standard input and output streams.

B. Concept of standard streams

Unix commands can communicate with one another using streams. Ten streams are available to the user, numbered 0 to 9. The first three of these streams are precisely defined:
- stream 0 is the standard input stream used by commands to obtain information
- stream 1 is the standard output stream for commands to transmit information
- stream 2 is an standard error stream, used by commands to transmit error messages

By default, each of these streams is associated with a peripheral:
- the standard input stream is associated by default with the keyboard
- the standard output stream is associated by default with the screen
- the standard error stream is associated by default with the screen

Information to be transmitted to a command is often stored in a file. Similarly, it is often desirable to keep the results produced by a command in a file. In addition, it is often useful to store any error messages produced by a process in a file, so as to analyze them later. To provide for all this, you can redefine or redirect the standard streams.

(kernel version 2.0 à 2.2)

C. Redirecting standard streams

First it must be noted that the redirection of a standard input, output or error stream is effective only during execution of the command with which they are associated. When execution of the command has finished, the redirection files are automatically closed and the standard streams return to their default definitions.

1. Redirecting output

The syntax of output stream redirection is as follows:
`n> file`

where n is the number of the redirected stream. To specify the redirection of the standard output stream you do not need to indicate its number (c.f. remark below). For example, to redirect the output of the **ls** command to the **tmp** file:

`ls > tmp` is equivalent to `ls 1> tmp`

Similarly, you can redirect the error stream to the **tmp** file as follows:

`ls 2> tmp`

> *If a file does not exist it is created: if a file does exist it is overwritten. The bash shell offers an option allowing you to prevent a file being overwritten in this way. This option is called* **noclobber**, *which is set using the command:*
> **set -o noclobber**
> *To inhibit the action of noclobber and overwrite anyway you must use a special redirection notation:*
> **ls >| tmp**

```
$ set -o noclobber
$ ls >f1
bash: f1: cannot clobber existing file
$ ls >| f1
```

🚩 *Redirection is implemented before the command. Consequently, if there is a syntax error in the command line, the command is not executed but the redirection file is still created and opened. This is because redirection operators are recognized and substituted by the shell while the command line is being parsed. As a result, the redirection is established before the command is executed.*

2. Adding items to the end of a file

The redirection file is closed once the command concerned has finished executing. A later output redirection to the same file will overwrite its contents. To redirect the output of a command to an existing file without overwriting its contents use the following redirection syntax:

```
ls 1>> tmp
```

In this case the output of **ls** is appended to the end of the tmp file. Again, you can omit the 1. If this file does not exist it is created.

3. Redirecting input

The syntax to redirect an input stream is the same as that for an output stream except that the > character changes direction:

```
n < file
```

To redirect the standard input stream you do not have to specify the number (0).

All of these streams can be redirected for the same command. For example, the command **wc** counts the number of lines, words and characters supplied by its input stream. The results are sent to the output stream. For example, to find out how many lines, words and characters there are in the **tmp** file and keep the results in the **res.txt** file, use the following syntax:

```
wc <tmp > res.txt
```

You can specify these redirections in any order, however you must be aware that the shell analyses a command line from left to right. It is very important to bear this in mind when redirecting or duplicating streams.

4. Duplicating streams

So far, we have seen redirections of streams to and from files, which are opened before execution and closed afterwards.

In addition, a stream can be redirected to, or duplicated as, another stream. This is done using the following syntax:

```
n>&m
```

which means that the n stream is duplicated as the m stream. If the m stream has previously been redirected to a file, the n stream will also be redirected (indirectly) to the same file.

As the shell analyses the command line from left to right, the two lines below are not equivalent:

```
cmd > tmp 2>&1
cmd 2>&1 >tmp
```

As has already been mentioned, the redirection file is closed just after execution of the command. However, you may wish to associate a file to the same stream of several commands. There are several ways of doing this:
- create the file by a redirection () then use append redirections (), repeating the file name each time with all the inherent risks of error in this filename.
- group commands together with braces {...} and apply the redirection to the group. This can cause problems when there are a certain number of commands in the group. The point of using braces {...} is to be able to execute a set of commands in the background, possibly grouping together the redirections.
- create a new stream by associating it to a file, then use a simple redirection to this stream for each of the commands concerned and close the file associated with the new stream at the end of the processing.
- create a script, then redirect the output on execution.

5. Opening a new stream

Simultaneously and in parallel to the three standard streams, the shell allows you to open seven other streams numbered 3 to 9.

To open stream 3, as an output for example, use the following syntax:

```
exec 3> tmp
```

This command opens stream 3 and associates it with the tmp file, which is either created and opened, or overwritten if it already exists.

Then, for each command, you can duplicate the output stream as this stream, using a simple redirection.

(kernel version 2.0 à 2.2)

Stream 3 stays open until its closure is specifically requested by duplicating it as the pseudo stream:

```
exec 3>& -
```

Once closed, a stream can be opened either as input or output.

The use of supplementary streams adds a lot more flexibility to redirections within a script. It necessitates neither double redirections, nor filenames (which can be troublesome to manage).

The redirection methods discussed above provide a first approach to getting commands to communicate with each other. Consider the following line:

```
cmd1 > tmp ; cmd2 < tmp
```

The output of the first command is redirected to the tmp file, which is used for redirecting the input of the next command.

Redirecting standard and supplementary streams provides a first form of communications between commands by redirecting the output of a command to a file and then using that file as the standard input of the next command.

However, it would be quicker and more efficient to be able to connect the output of one command directly to the input of the next command. And this is precisely what pipes allow you to do.

D. Connecting commands using pipes

This technique allows you to connect the output of a command to the input of the another command. In this way, the output byte stream of the one command becomes the input byte stream of the next.

A pipe can be considered as a virtual communications stream between two commands. It is denoted by the pipe character (I). It is a one-way stream without exchanges, simply transmission in one direction. In addition, the second command is dependent on the first command and waits for the bytes produced by it.

For example, take the **wc** command. The **-w** option will display only the number of words on its input stream. One way of finding out the number of files in your current working directory is to use the following pipeline:

```
Ls | wc -w
```

You can create a pipeline (a complex command using pipes) on three conditions:

① The result of the first command must be produced on its standard output. It cannot be a print command for example.

② Any intermediary commands must be filters. This means they must process bytes coming from their input stream and produce the result on their output stream.

③ The last command must have an input stream. It cannot be the **ls** command for example.

Further examples of pipelines can be seen throughout this book.

(kernel version 2.0 à 2.2)

Chapter 9

The vi editor principal commands

A. Why vi ? 108

B. Presenting vi 108

C. Moving around in the text 109

D. Correcting in command mode 110

E. Replacing characters or character strings . . 111

F. Searching for a character string 112

G. Copying and moving text 112

H. Command line mode: ex mode 113

I. Configuring the editor 114

A. Why vi ?

The vi editor (vi for visual) is the standard text editor delivered with all Unix systems. Its complexity is equaled only by its power and its flexibility which make it one of the most efficient editors on the market. vi also exists for other environments such as MS-DOS and even Windows NT.

However, there are other editors available, notably **emacs** which is just as powerful as **vi** and which you can configure in many different ways, to the extent that you can almost completely change its functioning.

Our objective is to provide the basic elements for you to edit a text file simply, rather than covering an editor in detail. For this reason we have chosen the vi editor as it is the one most commonly used on Unix and Linux. This is not a value judgement on the other editors, however, especially not on the graphical editors which use a more intuitive approach.

B. Presenting vi

The power mentioned above entails two drawbacks for the beginner:
– an old fashioned appearence
– a complexity that can be stressful when learning but which is quickly forgiven

However, we will present here only the basic commands that allow you to enter and modify text.

It is recommended that you read the on-line help to find out more and especially to experiment with each command, so as to benefit from all the power that vi has to offer.

(kernel version 2.0 à 2.2)

Chapter 9

This editor runs in two modes:
- Input, or text-entry, mode in which each character you type will be inserted on the screen
- Command mode in which each key you use corresponds to a particular command.

To go from input mode to command mode press [Esc].

How you go from command mode to input mode will depend on the type of insertion you require:

- **i** to insert text before the cursor
- **a** to insert text after the cursor
- **I** to insert at the beginning of the current line
- **A** to insert at the end of the current line
- **o** create a new line after the current line
- **O** create a new line before the current line

C. Moving around in the text

- **h*** one character to the left
- **l*** one character to the right
- **k*** one line up
- **j*** one line down
- **0** start of line
- **$** end of line
- **w*** next word
- **b*** previous word
- **fc*** go to the character "c" on the active line
- [Ctrl] **F** one screen up
- [Ctrl] **B** one screen down

The vi editor principal commands

Using Linux

    z `Enter` put the cursor in the line at the top of the screen
    z. put the cursor in the line in the middle of the screen
    G last line in the file
    nG go to the nth line. Example. 2G goes to the 2nd line

All commands indicated with a * can be prefixed with a number to indicate how many movements must be made. For example, **3fy** will move the cursor to the third occurrence of the character y to the right.

In addition to the keys described above, you can use the arrow keys, **PgUp** and **PgDn**.

D. Correcting in command mode

    x delete the character under the cursor
    X delete the character in front of the cursor
    rc replace the character under the cursor by the character "c"
    nx delete the next "n" characters
    dw delete the current word from the position of the cursor to the end of the word
    d$ (or D) delete all the characters from the cursor to the end of the line
    d0 delete all the characters from the cursor to the beginning of the line
    dfc delete all the characters on the active line up to the character "c"
    dG delete all the characters from (and including) the active line to the end of the text

(kernel version 2.0 à 2.2)

dnG delete all the characters from (and including) the active line up to the nth line

dd delete the active line

Similarly, you can prefix commands by a number to indicate the number of deletions to be made. For example, **10dd** will delete 10 lines starting from the active line.

E. Replacing characters or character strings

cw replace the current word, starting from the cursor

c$ replace from the cursor to the end of the line

c0 replace from the cursor to the beginning of the line

cfc replace from the cursor to the next occurrence of the character "c" on the line

c/xy [Enter] replace up to the next occurrence of the string "xy"

Once the replacement has been made, press [Esc] to complete the command.

As for other commands, these replacement commands can be prefixed by a number of occurrences.

F. Searching for a character string

/xy Enter search for the string "xy" forwards in the file
?xy Enter search for the string "xy" backwards in the file
n repeat the last search
N repeat the last search in the other direction

These commands accept regular expressions (Cf. Chapter 12). Consequently, it may be necessary to inhibit interpretation of special characters, by using the back-slash (\) character.

G. Copying and moving text

y + position copy the text from the cursor to the position indicated and transfer the copy to a buffer
d + position cut the text from the cursor to the position indicated and transfer it to a buffer
p paste the contents of the buffer behind the cursor
P paste the contents of the buffer before the cursor

These commands can be prefixed with a quotation mark and a lower-case letter so as to use one of the 26 memory buffers available.

(kernel version 2.0 à 2.2)

Here is an example:

`"sd/test` cuts the text from the current character to the next occurrence of the string "test" and transfers it to the buffer identified by the letter "s".

H. Command line mode: ex mode

These commands are called **ex** commands as they originate from an old Unix editor called ex. All these commands are prefixed by a colon (:) and must be confirmed by pressing Enter.

One of their advantages is that they appear on the bottom line of the screen.

:q   Leave the editor. If the memory contains information which has not yet been saved, a warning is displayed. The **:q!** command allows you to avoid this warning.

:x   Save the active file and leave the editor.

:w [file]   The contents of the memory buffer are saved in the specified file. If the file does not exist it is created, otherwise it is overwritten.

:ln1,ln2w [file]   The lines ln1 to ln2 are saved in the specified file.

:r file   The specified file is inserted in the memory buffer, at the active line.

:!command   The specified command is executed by the shell.

:r!command   The specified command is executed and the result is displayed after the active line. For example **:r!date** inserts the system date after the active line.

:f   The name of the active file and the active line number are displayed.

:e file   The specified file is loaded into memory. If the memory contains information which has not yet been saved a warning will be displayed. The **:e! file** command avoids display of this warning.

:e #   The last file loaded is called into memory. This is a simple method to switch between several files.

I. Configuring the editor

The **vi** editor has a certain number of options allowing you to adapt its functioning. You can view the list of these options along with their definitions using the **ex :set all** command.

```
autoindent         flipcase=""         number                      nosync
autoprint          nohideformat        nooptimize                  tabstop=4
autotab            noignorecase        paragraphs="PPppIPLPQP"     taglength=0
noautowrite        noinputmode         prompt                      tags="tags"
nobeautify         keytime=2           noreadonly                  tagstack
cc="cc -c"         keywordprg="ref"    remap                       term="vt100"
nocharattr         lines=24            report=5                    noterse
columns=80         nolist              noruler                     timeout
nodigraph          magic               nosafer                     warn
directory="/tmp"   make="make"         scroll=11                   window=0
noedcompatible     mesg                sections="NHSHSSSEse"       wrapmargin=0
equalprg="fmt"     nomodelines         shell="/bin/bash"           wrapscan
errorbells         more                showmatch                   nowriteany
noexrc             nearscroll=24       showmode
exrefresh          newfile             shiftwidth=8
noflash            nonovice            sidescroll=8
```

Here are some of the more commonly used of these options:

autoindent When a line is created, it adopts the indentation of the preceding line. This is used notably for programming.

number To display line numbers.

(kernel version 2.0 à 2.2)

showmatch This option is also used for programming. Each time a set of braces or brackets is closed, vi highlights briefly the corresponding opening brace or bracket thus allowing you to verify that you are closing what you think you are closing.

showmode Tells you which mode you are in with an indicator in the bottom right corner of the screen. This indicator can be either Input or Command.

tabstop=n Defines the number of spaces covered by a tab character.

To set an option use the **:set** command followed by the name of the option. To deactivate an option use the same command, prefixing **no** to the option name.

Setting examples:

```
:set showmode
:set number
```

Deactivation examples:

```
:set nonumber
:set noshowmatch
```

However, these settings or deactivations will be valid only during the vi session as they are stored only in memory.

To avoid having to configure vi manually every time you use it, a configuration file may be used. This file is called **.exrc** and must be present in your home directory. It contains the same setting and deactivation commands, but without the colons (:).

Here is an example of the **.exrc** file:

```
$ cat .exrc
set showmode
set tabstop=4
set number
set showmatch
set autoindent
```

Chapter 10

On-line help

A. On-line help 118

B. The man command 119

Using Linux

A. On-line help

In common with Unix, Linux has an extremely detailed on-line help facility. It is composed of eight main sections (their contents may differ slightly from the following list and other sections may also be present):

Section 1 details user commands

Section 2 concerns system calls

Section 3 presents library functions

Section 4 details special files

Section 5 defines the format of certain configuration files

Section 6 contains help on games present on the system

Section 7 contains macro packages and conventions

Section 8 concerns system management commands

Each of these sections resides in a directory called **man** suffixed with the section number and situated in the **/usr/man** directory.

```
/usr/man/man1
/usr/man/man2
/usr/man/man3
/usr/man/man4
/usr/man/man5
/usr/man/man6
/usr/man/man7
/usr/man/man8
```

(kernel version 2.0 à 2.2)

B. The man command

To obtain on-line help on a command, use the **man** command followed by the name of the command of interest. For example, **man ls** will display the help on the **ls** command contained in the **ls.1** file in the **/usr/man/man1** directory.

To find the file, the **man** command goes through the set of **man** directories searching for a file with the same name (before the extension) as the argument passed to the **man** command.

You must be careful, however, as the on-line help can contain two elements with the same name. For example **passwd** is not only a command but also a file. The file containing the on-line help of the **passwd** command is in the directory of the first section whilst that of the **passwd** file is in the directory of section 5. Which on-line help will Linux display in response to the command **man passwd**?

The order in which the various on-line help directories are searched is defined in the configuration file **/etc/man.config** or **/usr/lib/man.config**. In general, it is in the same order as the sections (1 2 3 4 5 6 7 8).

If you want to see the on-line help concerning the **passwd** file, you must indicate the section number to **man** explicitly, as follows:

```
man 5 passwd
```

The on-line help has a title, which is that of the item concerned with the section number in brackets. It is made up of several sections including (depending on the item concerned):

> **NAME** contains the name of the item concerned together with a brief description.
> **SYNOPSIS** describes the general syntax of a command.

DESCRIPTION provides a detailed description of the item concerned.
OPTIONS this section presents the full range of options available.
BUGS any functional problems or limitations are noted here.
AUTHOR, is sometimes presented
EXAMPLE
SEE ALSO gives other references.

(kernel version 2.0 à 2.2)

Chapter 11

Printing system

A. Overview 122

B. The BSD printing system 123

A. Overview

It is in printing and its management that the differences between the various Unix versions are most noticeable. This concerns both the command names and their functionalities. Three types of printing systems can be distinguished: BSD, System V and AIX.

We will limit ourselves here to the printing subsystems used by Linux. We will cover general aspects and those commands available to the user (to find out more, see the detailed presentation included in our book on Linux system administration).

A printing service is made up of the following elements:
- *printing commands* to request the printing of one or more files. BSD speaks of print *jobs* whilst System V and AIX use the term *requests*.
- spool *queues* to store requests and treat them sequentially
- *spool directories* containing requests in the form of files waiting to be printed
- *server processes* that transfer the requests from the spool directories to the printer.
- *administration commands* to start-up and stop the printing system and printer peripherals, manage queues and handle requests.

(kernel version 2.0 à 2.2)

B. The BSD printing system

This printing system is used by SunOS, IRIX, Digital Unix and Linux. It allows you to manage several local and remote printers and several spool queues. A set of four print commands are available:

lpr [filename]

This command requests the printing of a file for which the name is passed as an argument. It can also work from its standard input, which means that it is often connected to another command by a pipe. For example, to print the contents of the current working directory:

```
$ ls | lpr
$
```

This command adds the print request to the default printer spool queue. You can also decide to send the request to another printer. To do this occasionally, you can use the `-P PRINTERNAME` option of this command. If you wish to use another printer frequently, it is preferable to specify its name in the PRINTER environment variable. The printer specified in this way then becomes your default printer.

A certain number of options are available. Here is a selection of those most used:

- **-P** as mentioned above, this allows you to specify a printer other than that by default or that designated by the PRINTER variable
- **-m** tells you when the printing is finished, which can be useful depending on the length of the queue or the job.
- **-r** removes the file after printing.

-s instead of making a copy of the file, this option requests **lpr** to use the indicated file directly. This option is useful for large files. However, it is better not to modify its contents before the printing is finished.

-#n requests printing of n copies.

lpq

This command displays the list of print jobs currently in the print queues. Each job is assigned a job number.

```
$ lpr f1 f2
$ lpq
Rank     Owner      Job    Files         Total Size
1st      system     521    f1            15580 bytes
2nd      system     522    f2            16045 bytes
```

The above example shows the default printer spool queue. To display the spool queue for another printer, you can use the **-P** option followed by the name of the printer required.

One of the uses of this command is to find out the job number of a print request so as to delete it using the **lprm** command.

lprm
[job number]

This command removes the print job for a specified *job number*. Used without an argument, only the last job is removed. Used with an argument, all the specified jobs are removed from the spool queue of either the default printer, or that specified by the **-P** option.

```
$ lprm 521
dfA521Aa26534 dequeued
cfA521Aa26534 dequeued
```

(kernel version 2.0 à 2.2)

You may be wondering why two files have been dequeued when the removal of only one job was requested. The reason for this is that every job generates two files: a command file and another, which is a copy of the file you want to print. Therefore when a job is cancelled, both of these files must be deleted.

lpc [action]

This command displays information concerning the printers available on the system. This information indicates for each printer whether the spool queue is active and if the printer is in service. **lpc** is essentially an administration command. Its other actions are not accessible to users other than **root**.

This command functions either with an argument specifying the action to be carried out, or interactively, in which case it is possible to request several actions without leaving the command. The most useful sub-command is **status** which gives the status of the spool queue of the printer and the work in progress. The following example shows that the default printer is deactivated, but that the spool queue is still active. This means that users can continue to send requests which will be treated only when the printer is put back into service by the administrator. In the example, the system has two printers, the default printer called **lp** and another called **esps.** The latter allows you to print postcript documents and can be specified to **lpr** using the option -**P** esps .

```
$ lpc status
lp:
        queuing is enabled
        printing is disabled
        no entries
        no daemon present
esps:
        queuing is enabled
        printing is enabled
        no entries
        no daemon present
$ lpc
lpc status
lp:
        queuing is enabled
        printing is disabled
        no entries
        no daemon present
esps:
        queuing is enabled
        printing is enabled
        no entries
        no daemon present
lpc quit
$
```

(kernel version 2.0 à 2.2)

Regular expressions

A. Meta-characters 128

B. Special characters 129

A regular expression is a character string model that is useful for finding one or more character strings in a file without having to name them individually. Regular expressions can be used with the following commands: **grep**, **egrep**, **sed**, **awk**, **vi**, **ed** and **ex** (amongst others). . .

Regular expressions are constructed using special operators.

There are two types of special operator: meta-characters (which are characters used to designate other characters), and special characters (which allow you to specify a number of occurrences). In addition, the back-slash (\) character inhibits interpretation of special operators and allows them to be represented as themselves.

A. Meta-characters

The "." character matches any single character (not to be confused with the ? character which fulfils this function for the shell).

[. . .] matches any one of the characters specified between the square brackets. The character list is constructed using the same rules as for the shell, so that it can be stated explicitly or specified in the form of intervals. If the] must be included in the list it must appear immediately after the opening bracket ([). To specify a [; prefix it with \. All other meta-characters lose their special interpretation when between square brackets.

[^. . .] matches any character *not* included in the list following the ^ character (this is the equivalent of a ! for the shell).

(kernel version 2.0 à 2.2)

^ outside brackets represents the start of a line, whereas the $ character represents the end of a line. Thus ^$ represents a blank line.

B. Special characters

The * character matches zero, one or more consecutive occurrences of the character immediately preceding it. The preceding character can be represented by a regular expression.

You can specify a number of occurrences more precisely using the following notation:

\{n1,n2\} indicates that the character immediately preceding it can be present consecutively from n1 to n2 times. The preceding character can be represented by a regular expression.

\{n\} indicates that the character immediately preceding must be present consecutively n times.

\{n, \} indicates that the character immediately preceding it must be present consecutively at least n times.

In addition to the characters presented above, the **awk, grep** (with **-E** option) and **egrep** (POSIX standard) commands, use other special characters:

The + character indicates that the character immediately preceding it must be present consecutively at least once. It is therefore the equivalent of \{1,\}. Again the preceding character can be represented by a regular expression.

The ? character indicates that the character immediately preceding it must be present zero or one time. It can therefore be used instead of {0,1}. It must be noted that the braces {} are not preceded by the \ character. These must not be used with **egrep** or **awk** commands which are in conformity to the POSIX standard.

The | character You can indicate several alternatives, strings or regular expressions by separating them with this character.

Finally, you can group together several expressions, regular or not, by putting each of them between brackets. In this way they can be considered as an item for which a number of occurrences can be specified.

Example 1:

```
[A-Z][A-Z]*[-_.]txt
```

This expression matches any string containing at least one upper-case letter, followed by a dash, an underscore or a dot and ending with txt.

This expression could have been written as follows:

```
[A-Z]\{1,\}[-_.]txt
```

or

```
[A-Z]+[-_.]txt for awk or egrep.
```

Example 2:

```
^I'm going (to the | to) (garden?|Dover)$
```

(kernel version 2.0 à 2.2)

This expression matches a complete line made up of any of the following:
   I'm going to the garden
   I'm going to the gardens
   I'm going to Dover

Of course, this would also match "I'm going to the Dover", "I'm going to garden" or "I'm going to gardens".

Other examples will be given in the sections dealing with the **grep** and **egrep** commands.

↓ personal notes ↓

(kernel version 2.0 à 2.2)

Chapter 13

Handling files and directories

A.	Creating directories	134
B.	Deleting directories	136
C.	Copying files and directories	137
D.	Moving files and directories	139
E.	Deleting files and directories	140
F.	Viewing files and directories	141
G.	File types	145
H.	Creating files and modifying timestamps . . .	145
I.	Finding files and directories	147

Using Linux

When you log in for the first time, you go into an empty home directory. You then have to organize this directory to suit your needs by creating directories and subdirectories and by copying or moving files and maybe renaming them. In addition, you have to know how to move about, and to know where you are in the hierarchy at all times. You also have to know how to find out the contents of a directory, to locate files and to display information about them. These are all basic techniques for day to day working.

A. Creating directories

The **mkdir** command allows you to create a directory using the following syntax:

```
mkdir DIRECTORY
```

The directory will be created provided that you have the required permissions in the parent directory.

As this is a creation, the new directory's permissions will depend on the file creation mask. However, for various reasons, you may want wish to modify the default permissions assigned. To do this, use the **-m** option and supply the octal value of the permissions the new directory must have. With some systems, you can use the symbolic notation. This allows you to use the current mask as a basis and adapt it by adding or withdrawing permissions as required.

(kernel version 2.0 à 2.2)

Here is an example of the **mkdir** command with the **-m** option.

```
$ umask
077
$ mkdir dir1
$ mkdir -m 755 dir2
$ ls -l
total 2
drwx------   2 solo    users        1024 Feb  3 11:02 dir1
drwxr-xr-x   2 solo    users        1024 Feb  3 11:02 dir2
```

You may wish to create a set of nested directories, but if you attempt to do this without an option you will get an error message as follows:

```
$ mkdir dir3/dir4/dir5
mkdir: cannot make directory `dir3/dir4/dir5': No such file or directory
```

When invoked in this way, **mkdir** tries to create a new directory, **dir5,** in **dir4** which is itself in **dir3**. For **mkdir** to be successful, **dir3** and **dir4** must already exist. However, what we want to do is to create **dir3**, **dir4** and **dir5** at the same time. To provide for this, **mkdir** offers the **-p** option, which allows you to create a directory (**dir5** in this case) along with all the other directories necessary in the hierarchy (**dir3** and **dir4** in this case).

```
$ mkdir -p dir3/dir4/dir5
$ ls
dir1   dir2   dir3
$ ls dir3
dir4
$ ls dir3/dir4
dir5
```

The **dir5** directory will be created with permissions according to the file creation mask. Alternatively, permissions can be specified using the **-m** option which can be combined with the **-p** option. However, when the **dir3** and **dir4** directories are created, the default permissions may not be compatible with the ability to create a directory inside another one. The following example illustrates this:

```
$ umask 277
$ mkdir -p dir6/dir7
$ ls -l dir6
total 1
dr-x------   2 solo    users      024 Feb  3 11:20 dir7
$ ls -ld dir6
drwx------   3 solo    users     1024 Feb  3 11:20 dir6
```

In this example, the file creation mask has a value of 277 which means that directories will be created with owner read and execution permissions only. If **mkdir** uses this mask to create **dir6**, how can it then create **dir7**? In fact **mkdir** gets round this problem by adding the minimum permissions to allow it to carry out the required operation. In this case this means that write permission must be added for **dir6**. In conclusion, **dir7** is created with the default permissions and **dir6** is created with the default permissions plus owner write permission.

B. Deleting directories

To delete a directory use the **rmdir** command:

`rmdir DIRECTORY`

A directory can be deleted only if it is empty. In addition, the user invoking **rmdir** must have the required permissions to delete the directory or directories concerned.

In common with **mkdir, rmdir** offers the **-p** option, which allows you to delete any parent directories indicated, provided they are also empty.

(kernel version 2.0 à 2.2)

In the example below, **rmdir** refuses to delete the **dir6** directory because it is not empty; it contains the **dir7** directory. **rmdir** is used a second time to delete **dir7** and its parent directory with the **-p** option. The **ls dir6** command can only fail as **dir6** has just been deleted.

```
$ rmdir dir6
rmdir: dir6: Directory not empty
$ rmdir -p dir6/dir7
$ ls dir6
ls: dir6: No such file or directory
```

C. Copying files and directories

To copy files and/or directories, use the **cp** command. There are three different ways of using **cp**.

```
cp SOURCE_FILE DESTINATION_FILE
cp SOURCE_FILE DESTINATION_DIRECTORY
cp SOURCE_FILE_LIST DESTINATION_DIRECTORY
```

The first method gives you a copy of the file under another name.

The second method gives you a copy of the file with the same name but in a different directory.

The third method is an extension of the second: it copies a number of files to a destination directory, keeping the same file names. You cannot use **cp** to copy a list of files under different names as, in this case, the second argument of **cp** must be a directory, otherwise the command returns an error message.

In all cases, since the files have been created, the user becomes the owner of the files, the timestamp is filled in with the creation time and the permissions are assigned according to the value of the file creation mask.

```
$ umask 077
$ cp /etc/passwd .
$ ls -l /etc/passwd passwd
-rw-r--r--   1 root    root    1220 Jan 19 22:07 /etc/passwd
-rw-------   1 solo    users   1220 Feb  3 15:27 passwd
```

If a file of the same name is in the destination directory the file will be overwritten without warning (unless an alias has been installed which automatically implements the **-i** option: see below).

Several options allow you to modify the functioning of **cp**.

The **-i** option ensures that if a file of the same name is in the destination directory, a message will appear requesting permission to overwrite the file. Press **y** to overwrite or **n** to abandon the copy.

```
$ cp -i /etc/passwd .
cp: overwrite './passwd'? y
$
```

The **-p** option allows you to preserve as many of the file attributes as possible. This means that only the owner and the group will be modified. The permissions and dates will remain unchanged. It must be noted that the owner and the group will not be modified if the copy is carried out by **root**.

```
$ cp -p /etc/passwd ./users
$ ls -l /etc/passwd passwd users
-rw-r--r--   1 root    root    1220 Jan 19 22:07 /etc/passwd
-rw-------   1 solo    users   1220 Feb  3 15:27 passwd
-rw-r--r--   1 solo    users   1220 Jan 19 22:07 users
```

You can also copy a directory provided that you use the **-r** option. Here is the syntax concerned:

cp -r SOURCE_DIRECTORY DESTINATION_DIRECTORY

(kernel version 2.0 à 2.2)

D. Moving files and directories

On Linux a directory is a special type of file, which contains a list of files. The **ls -ld** command applied to a directory displays the size of the file list and not the space occupied by all the files contained in the directory. This latter function is provided by the **du** command.

Example:

```
$ ls -ld /etc
drwxr-xr-x   8 root     root     2048 Feb  3 11:00 /etc
$ du -s /etc
607      /etc
```

In the case of the /etc directory, its contents list occupies just over 2 kilobytes, whereas its contents occupy 607 kilobytes.

On Linux, the physical disk location of a file or directory bears no relation to that of its parent directory. A file hierarchy provides a logical organization of files and directories that is independent of the physical organization.

Consequently, to move a file or directory, all the system has to do is to modify the lists of the source and destination directories concerned. The execution time is totally independent of the size of the file or directory concerned. No item is created. All the system does to the file is to modify one of its attributes: its path if it moves to another directory, or its name if it stays in the same directory.

The only case where anything is created, and where the file creation mask is used, is when the destination disk is different from the source disk. It must be noted that in this case you cannot simply move a directory: you must first copy the directory, then delete the original directory.

To move or rename files and directories, you can use the **mv** command. The usage of **mv** is similar to that of **cp**:

```
mv SOURCE_FILE DESTINATION_FILE
mv SOURCE_FILE DESTINATION_DIRECTORY
mv SOURCE_FILE_LIST DESTINATION_DIRECTORY
```

As moving a directory is naturally recursive, **mv** does not have a **-r** option.

The two most useful **mv** options are the following:

- **-i** this has the same action as for **cp**, in that it requests confirmation to overwrite a file of the same name
- **-f** counters the **-i** option. This is useful when **mv** is automatically invoked with a **-i** option (using an alias for example).

E. Deleting files and directories

Files or directories are deleted using the **rm** command for which the syntax is as follows:

```
rm FILE(S)
```

The **rm** command does not request confirmation before deleting the file(s) or directory unless the **-i** option is used. It is therefore strongly recommended to define **rm** as an alias for 'rm -i' so as to activate this option by default. When you do not require this option for whatever reason, you can cancel it using the **-f** option, as for **mv**.

One of the most dangerous Linux commands is **rm** used with the recursive **-r** option. This deletes files and directories in all the subdirectories of the directory passed as an argument. The most devastating command for a user is:

```
rm -fr $HOME
```

(**Do not** try this to see what happens !)

(kernel version 2.0 à 2.2)

F. Viewing files and directories

Creating, deleting, moving and copying files and directories are the basic actions required to organize your work on a Linux system. However, such actions are often carried out according to the contents of certain directories or the presence of a file. You need to examine directory contents and you can do this using the **ls** command, one of the most commonly used on Linux. We have seen many examples of its use already without formally introducing it.

Used without option or argument, this command displays the contents of the current working directory:

```
$ cd /tmp
$ ls
fvwmrca01        fvwmrca25      lyx_tmp20912aaa  psdevtab
```

The **ls** command can be invoked with two types of argument: files and/or directories. There can be several arguments of several types: the functioning of **ls** adapts itself according to type:
- in the case of files, **ls** displays only their name.
- in the case of directories, their contents are displayed, provided that **ls** has the required permissions.

```
$ cd /
$ ls vmlinuz tmp passwd
/bin/ls: passwd: No such file or directory
vmlinuz

tmp:
fvwmrca01        fvwmrca25      lyx_tmp20912aaa  psdevtab
```

In this example **ls** was passed the names of a file, a directory and an unknown file. The error was indicated and the **vmlinuz** file name was displayed as present along with the contents of the **tmp** directory.

A large range of options allows you to adapt the functioning of **ls**. In fact, **ls** is one of the commands with the most options, around forty of them. Here is a selection of the most useful ones:

- **-a** displays all files and directories even those with names beginning with a dot (.), which are not listed by default.
- **-A** the same action as **-a** except that the special directories ./ and ../ are not displayed

```
$ ls -a
.               .X11-unix       .xisppipe.system   psdevtab
..              .XF86Setup1929  fvwmrca00161
.X0-lock        .s.PGSQL.5432   fvwmrca25461
$ ls -A
.X0-lock        .XF86Setup19    .xisppipe.system   fvwmrca25
.X11-unix       .s.PGSQL.5432   fvwmrca01          psdevtab
```

- **-c** sorts by last change time of file attributes, and shows this time when used with **-l**.
- **-d** lists the name of the directory passed as an argument instead of displaying the contents. This option is very useful, particularly when combined with **-l**.

```
$ ls /tmp
fvwmrca01       fvwmrca25       psdevtab
$ ls -d /tmp
/tmp
```

- **-i** displays inode numbers. These are indexes identifying files in relation to the disk or partition containing them.

```
$ ls -i
   13 fvwmrca01     16 fvwmrca25     15 psdevtab
```

- **-k** causes sizes to be displayed in kilobytes instead of 512-byte blocks (provided that the POSIXLY_CORRECT variable is set).

(kernel version 2.0 à 2.2)

-l displays information in long format for each file listed, including its type, permissions, number of physical links, name of owner, name of group, size in bytes, timestamp of last modification (except if **-c** or **-u** is used) and filename. In addition, the accumulated size of the items is displayed in kilobytes at the beginning of the list.

```
ls -l
total 78
-rw-------   1 system   users   32418 Feb 18 17:48 fvwmrca01
-rw-------   1 system   users   32418 Feb 21 23:41 fvwmrca25
-rw-rw-r--   1 system   users   12288 Feb 21 11:23 psdevtab
```

-n combined with **-l**, this option displays the **UID** of the owner and the **GID** of the group instead of their names.

```
$ ls -ln
total 78
-rw-------   1 504     100    32418 Feb 18 17:48 fvwmrca01
-rw-------   1 504     100    32418 Feb 21 23:41 fvwmrca25
-rw-rw-r--   1 504     100    12288 Feb 21 11:23 psdevtab
```

-r displays the contents of the directory in reverse order.

-s causes sizes to be displayed in 512 byte blocks instead of kilobytes (provided that the POSIXLY_CORRECT variable is set).

```
$ ls -s
total 78
  33 fvwmrca01      33 fvwmrca25      12 psdevtab
```

-t sorts the display by modification time, or by access time (if combined with **-u**), or by change time (last modification of file attributes - if combined with **-c**).

-u sorts by last access time, and shows this time when used with **-l**.

-1 lists in one column with just the filename (one per line).

```
$ ls -1
fvwmrca01
fvwmrca25
psdevtab
```

-F appends a character to the filename identifying its type:
* for an executable file
/ for a directory
= for a socket
@ for a link
| for a named pipe

```
$ ls -1AF
.X0-lock
.X11-unix/
.XF86Setup1929/
.s.PGSQL.5432=
.xisppipe.system|
fvwmrca01
fvwmrca25
usr@
psdevtab
```

(kernel version 2.0 à 2.2)

Chapter 13

G. File types

The **file** command displays the type (text file, executable, directory...) of one or more items of the file hierarchy.

The functioning principle of the **file** command is simple: it reads the first characters contained in the items concerned and determines their file type by consulting the **/etc/magic** file:

```
$ file .X11-unix fdes pipe usr psdevtab /bin/ls wtmp
.X11-unix:   directory
fdes:        socket
pipe :       fifo (named pipe)
usr:         symbolic link to /usr
psdevtab:    ascii text
/bin/ls:     ELF 32-bit LSB executable i386
(386 and up) Version 1
wtmp:        data
```

This Linux association file is one of the most advanced available: it contains over 1500 associations.

H. Creating files and modifying timestamps

The **touch** command is mostly used to create empty files. However, the real function of this command is to modify date/times of files. Every file has three times: the time it was last modified, the time it was last accessed and the time its attributes were last changed (owner, group, permissions).

The **touch** command allows you to modify the first two of these times, even though the file is not accessed and no modification is made to its contents.

Here is the syntax of the touch command:
```
touch [options] FILE
```

This command changes the last modification and last access times to the current time. If the file does not exist it is created empty. It is often used to create a file whose sole purpose is to provide a timestamp to indicate the beginning of an operation, such as archiving. In this way, only those files having times later than this timestamp will be taken into account in subsequent archiving operations.

The **touch** command has the following options:

- **-a** modifies only last access time
- **-c** does not create the file if it does not exist
- **-m** modifies only last modification time
- **-r** followed by the name of a file, times are updated using the times in this file instead of the current time
- **-t** allows you to specify a time to be used instead of the current time. This command is useful to make a file younger or older. Here is the format to be used for the time, which must follow the **-t**:
  - [[CC]YY]MMDDhhmm[.ss]
  - CC : century (e.g. 20 for 2001)
  - YY : year (e.g. 01 for 2001)
  - MM : month
  - DD : day
  - hh : hour
  - mm : minute
  - ss : seconds

The century, the year and the seconds are optional.

(kernel version 2.0 à 2.2)

I. Finding files and directories

You may need to find required files or directories before you can copy, move, delete or do anything else to them.

The **find** command allows you to search a set of directories for the files/directories corresponding to given criteria. Once the items have been found, **find** can carry out directly one or more operations on the files concerned, or simply display their names for use by another utility.

The **find** syntax structure is different from that of most Unix commands:

```
find PATH(S) CRITERIA [ACTIONS]
```

The search paths are separated from each other simply by a space.

Several forms of search criteria exist. Some of these are either infrequently used or of interest mainly to the system administrator. Here is a selection of criteria commonly used by the general user:

- **-type char** Search according to the type of item where **char** can be:
  - **f** for a regular file
  - **d** for a directory
  - **l** for a symbolic link
  - **b** for a special (buffered) block file
  - **c** for a special (unbuffered) character file
  - **p** for a named pipe
- **-name pattern** Search according to file name. You can use meta-characters in the pattern. However, you must protect them from interpretation by the shell, which must pass them on to **find** without interpreting them.

- **-size n** Search according to size. By default, the size is in units of 512-byte blocks. Suffix the size with a **c** to specify bytes, or with a **k** for kilobytes. Prefix with a **+** to request a search for a size greater than that indicated, or a **-** for a size less than that indicated. No prefix specifies a size exactly the same as that indicated.
- **-perm mode** Search according to permissions. Originally, only octal notations were accepted. However, modern versions of **find** accept symbolic notation.
- **-atime n** Search for files according to last access time.
- **-ctime n** Search for files according to time of last file status modification.
- **-mtime n** Search for files according to last modification time.

These last three criteria are specified in multiples of 24 hours since the event concerned. For example, **-mtime 1** specifies files modified more than 24 hours and less than 48 hours ago. The following notations can also be used:

```
-mtime +2 to specify files modified at least
48 hours ago
```

```
-mtime -2 to specify files modified less than
48 hours ago
```

Other criteria exist that are much more useful to the system administrator than to the general user.

By default, all criteria are cumulative so that **find** searches for files according to the complete set of specified criteria. If you wish to indicate alternative criteria, separate then with the **-o** "or" operator. You can also clarify the command using **-a** to specify the "and" operator explicitly.

(kernel version 2.0 à 2.2)

Once you have indicated the criteria, you may wish to specify actions to be undertaken on the files once they have been found.

By default, **find** displays the names of the files found. You can also specify this explicitly using **print**. If you wish to apply a Unix command to the files use the **-exec** option, according to the following syntax:

```
-exec command [options] {} \;
```

- **-exec** introduces the command followed by any options you wish to specify. The { } symbolizes the files concerned. You cannot specify these explicitly as they have not yet been found. The command is terminated with a semi-colon (;) protected by a back-slash (\). This prevents it being interpreted by the shell. Note the presence of a space between the closing brace (}) and the back-slash (\).
- **-ok** does the same thing as **-exec** except that confirmation will be requested before execution of your specified command. This can be useful for checking that your search criteria were properly defined or that the command to be executed is what you expected.

↓ *personal notes* ↓

(kernel version 2.0 à 2.2)

Chapter 14

Principal Linux commands

A.	Processing file contents	152
B.	Time Management	206
C.	Message commands	218
D.	Compressing files	226
E.	Process management	236

A. Processing file contents

One of the original objectives of Unix was to create a system to process text; from its input, to production of a printable file.

From the beginning, Unix was equipped with a large number of commands to handle file contents. As Unix makes no distinction between a byte stream and a file, these commands are mainly filters. As we mentioned previously, one of the characteristics of a filter is that it processes bytes provided on its input stream. Consequently, a file can be processed by a simple input redirection.

Displaying

    cat reads bytes from the input stream and displays them on the output stream
    head displays the first few lines of a file
    tail displays the last few lines of a file
    more reads bytes from the standard input and displays them on the terminal, with line management

Statistics

    wc displays the number of characters, words and lines on its input stream

Dividing and merging files

    split splits a file up into several files
    cat concatenates files
    join joins lines having common fields from two separate files
    paste merges lines from two files, one of which can be the standard input.

Sorting

    sort sorts the lines of a file

(kernel version 2.0 à 2.2)

Selective extraction

    grep extracts lines from a file that match a specified pattern

    cut extracts sections of lines from a file

Comparing files

    cmp simple comparison of the contents of two files

    diff advanced comparison of the contents of two files

    comm compares two sorted files, line by line

Miscellaneous processing

    uniq removes duplicated lines from a sorted file

    tr processes characters in a file

    expand converts tabs into spaces

    unexpand converts spaces into tabs

    fold wraps lines to fit into a defined width

    fmt simple line formatting, respecting words and indentation

    rev reverses the character order of each line

➔ **cat**

The **cat** command is a filter which reads bytes from its input stream and transmits them to its output stream. This filter has two main roles:
- to display the contents of small files
- to concatenate the contents of several files into one (as we shall see later).

As **cat** is able to read files directly, you do not have to use an input redirection technique.

```
$ cat exo1
I'm going
to the seaside
today
$ cat exo2
to take the car
because
it might rain
$ cat exo1 exo2
I'm going
to the seaside
today
to take the car
because
it might rain
```

cat is used to display the contents of files. It does not take terminal type into account and when all the file cannot fit on the screen only the last lines are visible. In order to view larger files more comfortably, utility programs are available that manage the display according to the type of terminal being used. On Unix, there are three such utilities: **more**, **pg** and **less**. **more** and **pg** are standard Unix commands. **less**, however, is a GNU program which is not present in all versions of Unix, but it is present on all Linux systems. **less** is very powerful and tends to be used instead of the other two commands.

→ **more**

more is one of the utility programs which allows you to display text (coming from a file or from the standard input) according to the terminal being used. This is useful when the text is made up of more lines that can fit on one screen. In this case, **more** displays as many lines as the screen can display, reserving the last line for information concerning the proportion of text displayed. It then waits for you to input a command.

Chapter 14

```
$ more /etc/profile
# commands common to all logins

export OPENWINHOME=/usr/openwin
export MINICOM="-c on"
export MANPATH=/usr/local/man:/usr/man/preformat:/usr/man:/usr/X11/
man:/usr/open
win/man
export HOSTNAME="`cat /etc/HOSTNAME`"
export LESSOPEN="|lesspipe.sh %s"
# netscape
export MOZILLA_HOME=/usr/local/netscape
# lclint
export LARCH_PATH=/usr/local/lib/lclint
# Wingz
export WINGZ=/usr/local/Wingz
PATH="$PATH:/usr/X11/bin:/usr/andrew/bin:$OPENWINHOME/bin:/usr/
games:.
LESS=-MM
# I had problems using 'eval tset' instead of 'TERM=', but you
might want to
# try it anyway. I think with the right /etc/termcap
it would work great.
# eval `tset -sQ "$TERM"`
if [ "$TERM" = "" -o "$TERM" = "unknown" ]; then
 TERM=linux
fi
--More--(45%)
```

Here are the commands you can use. You do not need to know them all, just enough to display the text comfortably. If you want to find out more about this command, you will find the manual page very instructive.

h or **?** is the only command you should not forget as it displays the **more** on-line help.

q, **Q** or [Ctrl]**C** allows you to exit from **more**.

v invokes the vi editor.

The following commands allow you to move around in the text. Some are the same as those used with **vi**. The number **k** is optional, its default value is indicated in each case. The ^ character followed by a letter signifies a key sequence with [Ctrl] pressed at the same time as the letter indicated:

> **k** [space]   displays the next screen or the next **k** lines.

kz displays the next screen or the next **k** lines. k then becomes the new default value for lines displayed by this command.

k [Enter] displays the next line or the next **k** lines.

kf skips forward to the next full screen or the **k**th next full screen. If the next screen is not a full one it is not displayed.

kb or **k^B** skips backward to the last full screen or the **k**th last full screen.

In addition, the [space] and [Enter] keys can be used to move quickly through the file. In common with **vi**, **more** offers commands to find character strings.

k/pattern searches for the next or the **k**th next occurrence of the regular expression indicated.

kn goes to the **k**th occurrence of the regular expression of the previous search.

' goes to where the previous search started.

Information commands:

= displays the current line number (that of the last line displayed on the screen).

:**f** displays the current file name and current line number.

Other commands:

^L Refreshes the screen. This can be useful when the screen has been disturbed, by the arrival of a mail message, for example.

(kernel version 2.0 à 2.2)

:n goes to the next file (or **k**th next file), provided that several files were specified when **more** was called.

:p goes to the previous file (or **k**th last file), provided that several files were specified when **more** was called.

In addition, **more** can be called with a certain number of options. Here are some of those more commonly used:

- **-d** displays with each prompt, the message [Press space to continue, 'q' to quit.], or [Press 'h' for instructions.] when you type a command that was not recognized.

- **-num** specifies a screen size **num** lines long.

- **+num** specifies the line number from which to start displaying.

- **+/ string** specifies a string that must be found in each file before it is displayed. If the string is found, display will start from this position.

If you want to use an option every time **more** is called and you cannot use an alias (if **more** cannot appear at the beginning of the command line), the MORE system variable is very useful:

```
$ export MORE="-d -5"
$ more tr.txt
1:town a
2:town a
3:town b
4:town c
5:town d
--More--(32%)[Press space to continue, 'q' to quit.]
```

→ head

The **head** utility displays the first lines read from its input stream. **head** displays 10 lines by default and the **-n** option allows you to display the first **n** lines.

Examples of head are given below:

```
[10]-system(merlin)~/cours/shell:head /etc/group
root::0:root,system,squid
bin::1:root,bin,daemon
daemon::2:root,bin,daemon
sys::3:root,bin,adm
adm::4:root,adm,daemon
tty::5:
disk::6:root,adm
lp::7:lp
mem::8:
kmem::9:system
[11]-system(merlin)~/cours/shell:ls |head -5
affidate
analyse
bin.aa.aa
bin.aa.old
bin.ab.12
```

→ tail

In contrast to **head**, **tail** displays the last lines read from its input stream, again 10 lines by default.

tail offers the following display options:

> **-n** displays the n last lines
>
> **+n** displays from line n to the end of the file

The **+n** option is useful to skip a certain number of header lines. For example, supposing that a file of 50 lines has 5 lines at the beginning that you do not want, you can use the following command:

```
tail +6 FILE > NEW_FILE
```

(kernel version 2.0 à 2.2)

➔ wc

This utility calculates and displays the number of lines, words and characters read on its standard input.

It must be noted that a line is defined by the presence of a newline character (ASCII code 10) and that words are defined by space separators.

You do not have to use the input redirection character with **wc**, as it can work with several files.

You can restrict the display to one or two statistics using the following options:

- **-l** displays the number of lines
- **-w** displays the number of words
- **-c** displays the number of characters

Here are a few examples of this command:

```
[16]-system(merlin)~/cours/shell:wc session
     11       45      226 session
[17]-system(merlin)~/cours/shell:wc -l session
     11 session
[18]-system(merlin)~/cours/shell:wc -wc session
     45      226 session
[19]-system(merlin)~/cours/shell:wc s*
     18       24      170 save.log
     41      120      859 archive
     11       45      226 session
      7       28      219 sort.txt
      8       32      312 sort1
      0        0        0 sort2
      7       28      273 sort2.txt
      0        0        0 sort3
     92      277     2059 total
[20]-system(merlin)~/cours/shell:cat session|wc
     11       45      226
```

wc displays these statistics on files whose names are passed as arguments. This allows **wc** to work with several files, displaying the results file by file with a totals line at the end.

As command 20 of the last example shows, you can avoid displaying a file name by using a pipe, although you cannot avoid displaying the file names of several files by direct usage of **wc**. However, you can do this by processing the result using the **cut** utility:

```
[21]-system(merlin)~/cours/shell:wc s*|cut -c-23
       18        24       170
       41       120       859
       11        45       226
        7        28       219
        8        32       312
        0         0         0
        7        28       273
        0         0         0
       92       277      2059
```

→ **split**

This utility splits up the lines of a file into several output files. By default, the first 1000 lines will be contained in the first output file called xaa, the next 1000 lines will be contained in the second output file called xab, etc. You can modify the number of lines that each output file will contain and also the prefix of output file names using the following syntax:

```
split [-n] [IN_FILE [OUT_FILE_PREFIX]]
```

The suffixes of the output files are made up of two letters starting from aa and continuing to zz, if necessary. If this is not sufficient, subsequent suffixes are composed of four letters following on from yz and starting with zaaa. In this way, concatenating the output files in sorted order would reconstitute the original input file.

(kernel version 2.0 à 2.2)

→ cat

As we have seen, **cat** allows you to display the contents of a file. As input redirection is implicit, it is possible to display the contents of several files. By redirecting the output to a file, you can concatenate these files into one: the inverse function of **split**.

Consequently, when **split** has produced several files whose names have a two-letter suffix, you can use **cat** to reconstruct the original file using the following command:

```
cat x??   FILE
```

→ join

This utility joins lines from two separate files having a common field. An SQL-type join is carried out . One of the two files can be the standard input, indicated by a dash (-).

Fields are separated by at least one space or one tab. Leading whitespace on a line is ignored. In addition, the two files must already have been sorted on the join field, so that these fields are in the same order in both files.

By default, the join is made on the first field of the first file. However, the option **-1 n** can be used to specify that the join must be made on the **n**th field of the first file, while the option **-2 m** specifies that the join must be made on the **m**th field of the second file.

By default, the result lines will be composed of the join field followed by the other fields of the two files. Lines not concerned by the join are not displayed.

```
$ head join[12]
== join1
Euston   Northern
Queensway   Central
Knightsbridge   Piccadilly
Bayswater   District
Blackfriars   Circle
Aldgate   Metropolitan
Angel
```

```
== join2
Northern   Black
Central    Blue
Piccadilly Green
District   Red
Circle     Brown
Metropolitan Violet
Bakerloo   Yellow

$ join -1 2 join1 join2
Euston       Northern     Black
Queensway    Central      Blue
Knightsbridge Piccadilly  Green
Bayswater    District     Red
Blackfriars  Circle       Brown
Aldgate      Metropolitan Violet
```

The following options are available with the **join** command:

-**a** n   to display unpairable lines of file n (either 1 or 2). These lines appear after the join display.

-**v** n   to display only unpairable lines of file n (either 1 or 2). The normal output (join) is not displayed.

-**t** char   to specify another character as the separator in both files.

-**o** list   to indicate a specific format for the output line. The list is made up of a series of m.n elements separated by spaces or commas, where m indicates the number of the file (1 or 2) and n is a positive integer indicating the field position in the file concerned.

-**e** string   to replace empty output fields (missing from the input) with the specified string. This option is often combined with -**o**.

(kernel version 2.0 à 2.2)

```
$ join -1 2 o 1.1  1.2  2.2  join1  join2
Euston   Northern  Black
Queensway  Central  Blue
Knightsbridge  Piccadilly  Green
Bayswater  District  Red
Blackfriars  Circle  Brown
Aldgate  Metropolitan  Violet

$ join -1 2 o 1.1  1.2  2.2  a1  -a2  join1  join2
Euston   Northern  Black
Queensway  Central  Blue
Knightsbridge  Piccadilly  Green
Bayswater  District  Red
Blackfriars  Circle  Brown
Aldgate  Metropolitan  Violet
Angel
Bakerloo Yellow

$ join -1 2 o 1.1  1.2  2.2  a1  -a2  -e '*****'  j
oin1  join2
Euston   Northern  Black
Queensway  Central  Blue
Knightsbridge  Piccadilly  Green
Bayswater  District  Red
Blackfriars  Circle  Brown
Aldgate  Metropolitan  Violet
Angel    *****  *****
*****    Bakerloo Yellow
```

→ **paste**

The **paste** utility concatenates, on the standard output, the lines of files passed as arguments. One of these files can be the standard input, indicated by the dash (-) character.

By default the input file lines are separated by a tab on the output.

```
$ cat exo1
I'm going
to the seaside
today
$ cat exo2
to take the car
because
it might rain
$ paste exo1 exo2
I'm going          to take the car
to the seaside     because
today     it might rain
```

paste has the following options:

-d to specify a list of separators. **paste** uses the first separator to separate lines coming from file 1 and 2, and the second separator to separate lines coming from file 2 and 3 and so on until the list is exhausted, after which it starts again at the beginning.

```
$ paste exo1 exo2
I'm going          to take the car
to the seaside     because
today     it might rain
$ paste -d " " exo1 exo2
I'm going to take the car
to the seaside because
today it might rain
$ paste -d " | " exo1 exo1 exo1
I'm going | I'm going | I'm going
to the seaside | to the seaside | to the seaside
today | today | today
$ paste -d "+-=" exo1 exo1 exo1
I'm going+I'm going-I'm going
to the seaside+to the seaside-to the seaside
today+today-today
$ paste -d "+-" exo1 exo1 exo1 exo1
I'm going+I'm going-I'm going+I'm going
to the seaside+to the seaside-to the seaside+to the seaside
today+today-today+today
```

(kernel version 2.0 à 2.2)

-s to concatenate the lines of one file at a time rather than concatenating one line from each file.

```
$ paste -s exo1 exo2
I'm going       to the seaside    today
to take the car because it might rain
$ paste -s -d" " exo1 exo2
I'm going to the seaside today
to take the car because it might rain
```

➔ **sort**

The **sort** command sorts lines of the file on its standard input. By default, lines are sorted in ascending order taking into account the whole of the lines.

Other sort modes are available:
- sort according to different fields, thus allowing multiple sort criteria.
- numerical sort
- sort in descending order

Here is the general syntax of the sort command:
```
sort [options] FILE
```

Here are the main sort options:

-d sorts in telephone-directory order. Only letters, digits and blanks are recognized. Other characters are ignored

-n sorts numerically. **sort** tries to convert the contents of each field to a numerical value (cf. example later on in this section).

-b ignores leading blanks in fields

-f lower-case letters are converted to upper-case letters when sorting so that no distinction in upper and lower case letters is made (case insensitive).

-r sorts in descending order

-t c uses the character 'c' as a field to locate the sort keys in each line.

```
$ cat sort.txt
Robert      Preston     442    66/10/26
Damien      Reading     355    72/09/12
Leonard     Salisbury   670    70/12/03
Leonard     Salisbury   670    72/05/14
Leonard     Reading     355    71/12/14
Lara        Brighton    339    67/04/01
Gina        Aldershot   167    64/08/30
Gerard      Salisbury   670    70/05/01

$ sort sort.txt
Damien      Reading     355    72/09/12
Gerard      Salisbury   670    70/05/01
Gina        Aldershot   167    64/08/30
Lara        Brighton    339    67/04/01
Leonard     Reading     355    71/12/14
Leonard     Salisbury   670    70/12/03
Leonard     Salisbury   670    72/05/14
Robert      Preston     442    66/10/26
```

In the example above, the first command displays the original file contents, which will be used for the subsequent examples. The second command carries out a default sort on this file. As the output is not redirected it appears on the screen.

It must be remembered that the sort is done line by line with the whole line being used as the sort key. Also, the characters are sorted according to their ASCII code. Thus, for the first line of the output there is no ambiguity, comparison of the first character is sufficient. However, since the next two output lines both start with the letter G, a decision could be made only after comparing second characters.

Concerning the lines 5, 6 and 7 (all beginning by Leonard), comparison must continue further along the line. Line 5 appears first because the "space" character in the tenth position has an ASCII code less than the S character. Discrimination between lines 6 and 7 is based on year-units of the birth-date. It is important to understand here that the digits

(kernel version 2.0 à 2.2)

are considered as characters and not as numerical values (we will come back to this later).

The following example illustrates the **-r** option:

```
$ sort -r sort.txt
Robert       Preston    442    66/10/26
Leonard      Salisbury  670    72/05/14
Leonard      Salisbury  670    70/12/03
Leonard      Reading    355    71/12/14
Lara         Brighton   339    67/04/01
Gina         Aldershot  167    64/08/30
Gerard       Salisbury  670    70/05/01
Damien       Reading    355    72/09/12
```

We will now look at multi-criteria sorts.

The sort keys can be defined in two ways: the first way we will look at is tending to become obsolete in favor of the second. Nevertheless, both of these methods use the concept of fields. For the **sort** command, fields are separated by spaces and tabs. However, unlike the **cut** command, only the first character is used as a separator: the others are considered to be part of the next field. If a file is composed of fields but separated by another character (as for the /etc/passwd file, for example), this must be indicated using the **-t** option followed by this character.

First method:

+pos1 [-pos2]

The +pos1 argument indicates the number of the field to be used as the start of the key, starting from zero. The -pos2 argument defines the number of the field after the end of the sort key (again starting from zero). In the absence of -pos2, the sort key would extend until the end of the line. Thus, to sort sort.txt according to the internal telephone extensions, **sort** must be told that the sort key begins with field 2 (telephone number), and that field 3 (birth-date) *(exclusively)* marks the end of the sort key. This gives the following command:

```
$ sort +2 -3 sort.txt
Gina        Aldershot    167    64/08/30
Lara         Brighton    339    67/04/01
Damien        Reading    355    72/09/12
Leonard       Reading    355    71/12/14
Robert        Preston    442    66/10/26
Gerard      Salisbury    670    70/05/01
Leonard     Salisbury    670    72/05/14
Leonard     Salisbury    670    70/12/03
```

Even though the result is what was expected, **sort** did not use digits alone in its calculation. There are three " space " characters between the town and telephone-number fields. The first is used as a separator, while the next two spaces are part of the telephone-number field.

As long as there is an identical number of spaces at the beginning of telephone-number field, this causes no problems; if this is not the case, the result can be surprising. In the next example we ask **sort** to use the town field as a sort key:

```
$ sort +1 -2 sort.txt
Gina        Aldershot    167    64/08/30
Robert        Preston    442    66/10/26
Damien        Reading    355    72/09/12
Leonard       Reading    355    71/12/14
Lara         Brighton    339    67/04/01
Gerard      Salisbury    670    70/05/01
Leonard     Salisbury    670    72/05/14
Leonard     Salisbury    670    70/12/03
```

The town field starts by a number of spaces which varies from line to line. As these characters are used in the sort, it is normal that the command may not work as we expected. In this case, you must use the **-b** option which requests **sort** to ignore leading spaces in the field, so that everything will work as intended:

(kernel version 2.0 à 2.2)

```
$ sort -b +1 -2 sort.txt
Gina       Aldershot   167    64/08/30
Lara       Brighton    339    67/04/01
Robert     Preston     442    66/10/26
Damien     Reading     355    72/09/12
Leonard    Reading     355    71/12/14
Gerard     Salisbury   670    70/05/01
Leonard    Salisbury   670    72/05/14
Leonard    Salisbury   670    70/12/03
```

Second method:

The second method involves defining the sort key using the **-k** option with the following syntax:

`-k pos1[,pos2]`

Intuitively, this method is easier to understand, and is tending to make the first method obsolete.

```
$ sort -k 3,3 sort.txt
Gina       Aldershot   167    64/08/30
Lara       Brighton    339    67/04/01
Damien     Reading     355    72/09/12
Leonard    Reading     355    71/12/14
Robert     Preston     442    66/10/26
Gerard     Salisbury   670    70/05/01
Leonard    Salisbury   670    72/05/14
Leonard    Salisbury   670    70/12/03
```

The correct specification is indeed **k 3,3** and not **k 3,4**. The fields are numbered from 1 and pos2 indicates the end of the sort key *inclusively*. Let us see what happens if we specify **k 3,4**:

```
$ sort -k 3,4 sort.txt
Gina       Aldershot   167    64/08/30
Lara       Brighton    339    67/04/01
Leonard    Reading     355    71/12/14
Damien     Reading     355    72/09/12
Robert     Preston     442    66/10/26
Gerard     Salisbury   670    70/05/01
Leonard    Salisbury   670    70/12/03
Leonard    Salisbury   670    72/05/14
```

In this example, the sort key starts at the beginning of field 3 and ends at the end of field 4. The result is not the same as the birth-dates are taken into account, notably for those lines with telephone extensions 670 and 355.

Even with this notation, you have the same problem of leading spaces in the field. Again, you may need to use the **-b** option.

In the next example, we will attempt to sort the lines of the sort2.txt file on the second field, in descending order. It must be noted that the fields in this file are separated by the ':' character. This must be indicated to **sort** using the **-t** option:

```
$ sort -t: -r -k 2,2 sort2.txt
news:9
mail:8
halt:7
nobody:65535
shutdown:6
sgbd:507
toto:506
soloc:505
system:504
grass:503
solob:502
soloa:501
sync:5
ftp:404
lp:4
adm:3
daemon:2
postmaster:14
man:13
operator:11
squid:1052
webuser:1051
webroot:1050
uucp:10
bin:1
root:0
```

(kernel version 2.0 à 2.2)

This is clearly not the result we expected. This is simply because the digits are considered as character strings and not as numerical values. To persuade **sort** to consider them as numerical values, the **-n** option must be used:

```
$ sort -t: -r -n -k 2,2 sort2.txt
nobody:65535
squid:1052
webuser:1051
webroot:1050
sgbd:507
toto:506
soloc:505
system:504
grass:503
solob:502
soloa:501
ftp:404
postmaster:14
man:13
operator:11
uucp:10
news:9
mail:8
halt:7
shutdown:6
sync:5
lp:4
adm:3
daemon:2
bin:1
root:0
```

You can also define several keys and use them to carry out a multi-key sort. This works as follows: first the list is sorted using the first key specified (primary key). Any lines which the primary key could not differentiate are then sorted by the second key; any lines which the second key could not differentiate are then sorted by the third key...

In addition, you can sort in ascending order (by default) on one key and sort in descending order on a secondary key. This is done using flags which are nothing other than options suffixed to field identifiers, as can be seen in the following example:

```
$ sort -b -k 2,2 -k 4r,4 sort.txt
Gina       Aldershot    167    64/08/30
Lara       Brighton     339    67/04/01
Robert     Preston      442    66/10/26
Damien     Reading      355    72/09/12
Leonard    Reading      355    71/12/14
Leonard    Salisbury    670    72/05/14
Leonard    Salisbury    670    70/12/03
Gerard     Salisbury    670    70/05/01
```

This command sorts the **sort.txt** file in ascending order on the second field. Those lines with similar second fields are sorted in descending order on the fourth field.

It must be noted that *options* have a general action on the command, and *flags* act only with respect to the key to which they are suffixed.

For some versions of **sort**, the presence of flags inhibit the action of a general option on the key concerned. Suppose we want to sort the lines of the same file on the towns in descending order, then apply a secondary sort on the telephone extensions in ascending order. We might try running the following command:

```
$ sort -b -k 2r,2 -k 3,3 sort.txt
Gerard     Salisbury    670    70/05/01
Leonard    Salisbury    670    72/05/14
Leonard    Salisbury    670    70/12/03
Lara       Brighton     339    67/04/01
Damien     Reading      355    72/09/12
Leonard    Reading      355    71/12/14
Robert     Preston      442    66/10/26
Gina       Aldershot    167    64/08/30
```

(kernel version 2.0 à 2.2)

The result is not as we expected, as Brighton is not where we expected it to be. The is because the action of the **-b** option is cancelled by the presence of the **-r** flag. To reactivate this option, it must be transformed into a flag, to give the following command:

```
$ sort -b -k 2br,2 -k 3,3 sort.txt
Gerard     Salisbury    670    70/05/01
Leonard    Salisbury    670    72/05/14
Leonard    Salisbury    670    70/12/03
Damien       Reading    355    72/09/12
Leonard      Reading    355    71/12/14
Robert       Preston    442    66/10/26
Lara        Brighton    339    67/04/01
Gina       Aldershot    167    64/08/30
```

The **-b** option was specified for its action on the second field. However, this option is effective only in the absence of a flag applied to this key. If no other flag is applied to the key, you can apply etiher the **-b** option or the **-b** flag.

Keys do not necessarily have to be defined by whole fields. You can also specify parts of fields. We will illustrate this using the second method (although this is also possible using the first method):

```
-k pos1.char1, pos2.char2
```

Here is an example of this technique:

```
$ sort -b -k 2,2 -k 4.3bnr,4.5 sort.txt
Gina       Aldershot    167    64/08/30
Lara        Brighton    339    67/04/01
Robert       Preston    442    66/10/26
Leonard      Reading    355    71/12/14
Damien       Reading    355    72/09/12
Leonard    Salisbury    670    70/12/03
Gerard     Salisbury    670    70/05/01
Leonard    Salisbury    670    72/05/14
```

This command requests a sort on the town field, with a secondary, descending, sort on the month of birth. As the month is numeric, this is indicated as a flag rather than a global option, which would have been cancelled out by the other flags. It must be noted also that the flag **b** requests **sort** to ignore leading spaces in the field. If this flag had not been included, the result would have been quite different.

```
$ sort -b -k 2,2 -k 4.3nr,4.5 sort.txt
Gina       Aldershot    167    64/08/30
Lara        Brighton    339    67/04/01
Robert       Preston    442    66/10/26
Damien       Reading    355    72/09/12
Leonard      Reading    355    71/12/14
Leonard    Salisbury    670    72/05/14
Gerard     Salisbury    670    70/05/01
Leonard    Salisbury    670    70/12/03
```

In this case, **-k 4.3nr,4.5** specifies the year and not the month of birth. This is because the field starts on the **tens** of years of birth, as the two leading spaces of the field are taken into account.

In conclusion, in spite of a syntax that may sometimes appear obscure and meticulous to use, the **sort** command allows you to carry out all kinds of sort, going well beyond the few examples we have presented in this section.

We will now look at two selective extraction commands. **grep**, which extracts lines according to whether or not they contain a character string supplied as an argument, and **cut** which extracts parts of lines according to column or field position.

➔ **grep**

Here is the **grep** general syntax:

grep [option] STRING

By default, **grep** reads the lines on its input stream and displays on its output stream those lines which contain the character string passed as an argument. In common with most commands covered in this chapter, **grep** is also a filter and you can redirect its input/output.

Here is a simple example which extracts the lines containing the string 'Salisbury' in the file **sort.txt**:

```
$ grep Salisbury sort.txt
Leonard     Salisbury    670    72/05/14
Leonard     Salisbury    670    70/12/03
Gerard      Salisbury    670    70/05/01
```

When **grep** searches in several files, each displayed line is prefixed by the name of the file from which it was extracted:

```
$ grep system /etc/passwd /etc/group
/etc/passwd:system:x:504:100:,,,:/home/system:/
bin/bash
/etc/group:root::0:root,system,squid
/etc/group:kmem::9:system
/etc/group:wheel::10:root,system
/etc/group:floppy::11:root,system,webroot
/etc/group:uucp::14:uucp,system
/etc/group:operator::16:root,system
/etc/group:users::100:games,system
/etc/group:sgbd::105:system
/etc/group:squid::20:root,system
```

Here are the main **grep** options:

- **-c** indicates the number of lines containing the specified string.
- **-h** suppresses the filename prefix when searching in several files
- **-i** ignores uppercase/lowercase distinction (i. e case insensitive)
- **-l** outputs only the names of the files in which the string was found
- **-n** prefixes each output line with its input-file line number

-**v** outputs the lines *not* containing the specified string

-**x** outputs only those lines for which the whole line matches the specified string (you can also specify this criterion in the regular expression of the string to match).

The **egrep** command is an extended form of **grep** allowing you to specify, amongst other things, several alternative strings separated from each other by the '|' pipe character. Here is an example of this command:

```
$ egrep "Reading|Leonard" sort.txt
Damien       Reading     355    72/09/12
Leonard      Salisbury   670    72/05/14
Leonard      Salisbury   670    70/12/03
Leonard      Reading     355    71/12/14
```

It must be understood that, in reality, **egrep** is a symbolic link to **grep** which emulates the functioning of the old Unix **egrep**, before it was POSIX standardised. However, egrep does not support the full use of regular expressions. Consequently, it is preferable to use **grep** with the **-E** option. You can, of course, create an alias egrep= "grep -E" in order to simulate the **egrep** command in conformity with the POSIX standard.

➔ cut

The **cut** command is used to extract sections of lines from the input stream. These sections can be defined by column positions, or fields indicated by their number. By default, fields are separated by tab characters.

(kernel version 2.0 à 2.2)

To extract characters, use the **-c** option followed by the column positions concerned. These numbers can either be specified as an exhaustive list, separated by commas (,), or by intervals indicating the first and last position separated by a dash (-). The two **cut** commands in the next example return the same results:

```
$ cat cut.txt
Robert          Preston     442     66/10/26
Damien          Reading     355     72/09/12
Leonard         Salisbury   670     70/12/03
Leonard         Salisbury   670     72/05/14
Leonard         Reading     355     71/12/14
Lara            Brighton    339     67/04/01
Gina            Aldershot   167     64/08/30
Gerard          Salisbury   670     70/05/01
$ cut -c 1-8 cut.txt
Robert
Damien
Leonard
Leonard
Leonard
Lara
Gina
Gerard
$ cut -c 1,2,3,4,5,6,7,8 cut.txt
Robert
Damien
Leonard
Leonard
Leonard
Lara
Gina
Gerard
```

If the file is made up of fields of unequal length, as with the **cut.txt** file above, it is easier to extract the fields using their field number rather than specifying character positions. In this case, use the **-f** option followed by the field number. These numbers can be specified in the same way as character positions.

As has already been mentioned, for **cut**, fields are separated by tabs by default. If fields are separated by several tabs, the superfluous characters must be deleted using the **tr** command (described later in this chapter). If another separator is used, you can indicate it with the **-d** option as in the following example:

```
$ cat cut2.txt
root\0\root
bin\1\root,bin,daemon
daemon\2\root,bin,daemon
sys\3\root,bin,adm
adm\4\root,adm,daemon
tty\5\
disk\6\root,adm
lp\7\lp
mem\8\
kmem\9\
wheel\10\root
floppy\11\root
mail\12\mail
news\13\news
uucp\14\uucp
man\15\man
users\100\games
nogroup\-2\
stage01\50\
sgbd\110\
$ cut -d'\' -f2 cut1.txt
0
1
2
3
4
5
6
7
8
9
10
11
12
13
14
15
100
-2
50
110
120
```

Comparing files

→ **cmp**

This command allows you to compare two files of any type. You can use it, not only with text files, but also with binary files. One of the two files can be specified as a dash (-), indicating the standard input.

If the command terminates without a message, it means that the two files are identical. Otherwise, **cmp** indicates the first line and character position where the two files differ.

```
$ head -1 f1 f2
==> f1 <==
#!/bin/ksh

==> f2 <==
#!/bin/sh
$ cmp f1 f2
f1 f2 differ: char 8, line 1
```

The first command displays the first line of files f1 and f2, showing that they differ on the eighth character. This is confirmed by the **cmp** command.

By default, the objective of **cmp** is to check whether or not two files are identical. The **-l** option allows you to list any differences. Each element of this list is composed of the byte-number where a difference is found, followed by the octal byte-value in the two files.

```
$ cmp -l f1 f2
    8 153 163
    9 163 150
   10 150  12
   11  12  43
   13 167  43
   14 150  40
   15 151 103
   16 154 141
   17 145 154
   18  40 143
   19  72 165
   20  12 154
   21 144  40
   22 157 144
   23  12 165
   24  11  40
   25 163 156
   26 154 157
   27 145 155
   28 145 142
   29 160 162
   30  40 145
   31  61  40
   32  12 144
   33 144 145
   34 157  40
   35 156 143
   36 145 141
   37  12 162
cmp: EOF on f1
```

The message **cmp : EOF on f1** means that the command reached the end of **f1** before it reached the end of **f2** (this alone would have been sufficient to tell you there was a difference between the two files, but then this is only an example!).

➜ **comm**

The **comm** utility compares previously sorted files, for which the names are passed as arguments. A dash (-) instead of a filename specifies the standard input.

By default, the result is presented in three columns. The first indicates lines present only in the first file, the second indicates lines present only in the second file and the third indicates lines that are common to both files.

```
$ paste f1 f2
1           1
2           2
3           3
4           4
5           5
6           6
7           8
9
$ comm f1 f2
                        1
                        2
                        3
                        4
                        5
                        6
7
            8
9
```

You can inhibit the display of any or all of these columns using the option **-1** so as to omit column 1, **-2** to omit column 2 and **-3** to omit column 3. Thus the command **cmp -123 f1 f2** displays nothing. This saves you using the /dev/null redirection, which has the same effect.

➔ **diff**

The **diff** command constructs a list of differences between files in such a way as to indicate the modifications to be applied to the first file for it to become identical to the second. **diff** is an extremely powerful utility, which is able to base itself on identical lines, even if these lines are not in the same position in both files.

The required modifications are indicated as follows:
− a line number of the first file may be followed by a second line number, separated by a comma (,).
− an action code: **a** for add, **d** for delete or **c** for change

This allows three types of modification:

n1an2,n3 The lines **n2** to **n3** of the second file must be added after the line **n1** of the first file. There may be only one line to add in which case **n3** will not appear. The lines **n2** to **n3** of the first file are displayed, each prefixed with a > character.

n1,n2dn3 The lines **n1** to **n2** of the first file must be deleted as they are absent from the second file. There may be only one line to delete in which case **n2** will be omitted. The lines **n1** to **n2** of the first file are displayed, each prefixed with a < character.

n1,n2cn3,n4 The lines **n1** to **n2** of the first file must be replaced by the lines **n3** to **n4** of the second file. According to the required modifications, the line numbers **n2** and/or **n4** may be omitted. The lines **n1** to **n2** of the first file are displayed, each prefixed with a < character, followed by the lines **n3** to **n4** of the second file, each prefixed with a > character.

(kernel version 2.0 à 2.2)

Chapter 14

The following example illustrates **diff** working with two files, **ls1** and **ls2** (produced by the **ls** command):

```
$ diff ls1 ls2
2d1
< analyse
5d3
< bin.ab.ab
6a5
> bin.ab.ab
20d18
< cdenews
23c21,40
< diff1
---
> exo.lyx
> exo1
> grep.txt
> job1
> job2
> job3
> job4
> joba
> jobb
> jobc
> list_fct.c
> sort.txt
> sort1
> sort2
> sort3
> toto
> vi.sub
> analyse
> bin.ab.ab
> cdenews
31,34d47
< grep.txt
< joba
< jobb
< jobc
38a52,53
> jobb
> jobc
43d57
< list_fct.c
51d64
< sort2
```

Using Linux

The **diff** utility offers an impressive number of options. Amongst the most useful are those which allow you to adapt the processing:

-**b** ignores differences in the amounts of white space (spaces and tabs). With this option, if two files differ only by these characters they will be considered identical.

```
$ head diff2.2 diff2.3
==> diff2.2 <==
affidate
bin.aa. aa
bin.aa.old

==> diff2.3 <==
affidate
bin.aa.        aa
bin.aa.old
$ diff diff2.2 diff2.3
2c2
< bin.aa. aa
---
> bin.aa.        aa
$ diff -b diff2.2 diff2.3
$
```

It must be noted that **diff -b** does not ignore space and tab characters. It simply ignores any differences in the numbers of these characters, as long as they are present in corresponding positions of both files. **diff -b** will react if it finds such characters present in one file, and totally absent in the corresponding place in the second file:

(kernel version 2.0 à 2.2)

```
$ head diff2.2 diff2.4
==> diff2.2 <==
affidate
bin.aa. aa
bin.aa.old

==> diff2.3 <==
   affidate
bin.aa.     aa
bin.aa.old
$ diff -b diff2.2 diff2.3
1c1
< affidate
---
>    affidate
```

To ignore whitespace differences completely, use the **-w** option.

- **-i** ignore uppercase/lowercase differences (ie. case insensitive).

- **-q** indicates only if the files differ, without providing details of the differences.

```
$ diff -q diff2.2 diff2.3
Files diff2.2 and diff2.3 differ
```

- **-r** to compare recursively any subdirectories found (when comparing two directories). With this option, **diff** will process recursively two directories passed as arguments, by comparing files present in the two directories. It must be noted that **diff** does not compare the contents of the directories; it compares only the contents of the *files* contained in the two directories.

- **-s** In contrast to **-q**, this option indicates if the two files are identical. If they are not, **diff** functions as usual.

```
$ diff -s diff2.2 diff2.3
2c2
< bin.aa. aa
---
> bin.aa.    aa
$ diff -bs diff2.2 diff2.3
Files diff2.2 and diff2.3 are identical
```

-w ignores whitespace characters completely. The following example illustrates the difference between this option and **-b** which does not take into account differences in numbers of occurrences of spaces and tabs as long as there is at least one in the corresponding places of both files. The **-w** option simply ignores these characters when comparing the two files:

```
$ diff -b diff2.2 diff2.4
1c1
< affidate
---
>    affidate
$ diff -w diff2.2 diff2.4
$ diff -ws diff2.2 diff2.4
Files diff2.2 and diff2.4 are identical
```

The results provided by **diff** are very rich, but the modifications it suggests still have to be correctly implemented. However, **diff** offers two further options which format the results in such a way that they can be interpreted directly by existing utilities.

The first of these options is **-e** which produces a script that **ed** can use to apply the transformations directly to the second file, so that it is identical to the first in all respects. However, an instruction must be added to the end of the file written by **diff** so that the results contained become fully useable. This in itself is not a major handicap. The main difficulty lies in the fact that you cannot process two *directories* in the same way.

Chapter 14

Although **diff** is able to provide transformation instructions which can be applied to the files of a second directory so that they are identical to the first, these results cannot be directly interpreted by **ed** unless they are integrated into a script.

The **-c** option produces particularly useful results, especially since they can be used directly by the **patch** utility, which is able to apply them recursively to a complete file hierarchy. We will illustrate this powerful Linux tool in the next section which covers the **patch** utility.

```
$ head patch2.2 patch2.3
==> patch2.2 <==
affidate
bin.aa. aa
bin.aa.old
extra line (2.2)

==> patch2.3 <==
supplement
affidate
bin.aa.     aa
bin.aa.old
$ diff -c patch2.2 patch2.3
*** patch2.2    Mon Mar  1 11:38:59 1999
--- patch2.3    Mon Mar  1 11:39:05 1999
***************
*** 1,4 ****
  affidate
! bin.aa. aa
  bin.aa.old
- extra line (2.2)
--- 1,4 ----
+ supplement
  affidate
! bin.aa.     aa
  bin.aa.old
```

With the **-c** option, **diff** outputs the results differently from its standard presentation:
- a header is displayed indicating the names of the two files, followed by the differences in the two files set in their respective contexts. This is done by including context lines.

— These lines are identical in both files and appear immediately before and after the differences. In the above example, the context line are:
```
affidate
```
and
```
bin.aa.old
```
— context lines are presented with two leading spaces. Lines which differ from one file to the other are prefixed by one of the following indicators:

- for a line which must be deleted from the first file because it is absent in the second,

+ for a line that is present in the second file and absent in the first,

! for a line present in the context (line sequence) of both files, but which differs from one file to the other.

Quite apart from differences in presentation of the -c option, the advantages offered by this format are immediately apparent. It contains the names of the files to which the modifications apply. This allows you to process the directories by applying the **patch** utility directly to the same modification file (the **patch** utility is described later on in this chapter).

Another format exists, called the unified format, which contains the same information but in a more compact form. It enables you to produce smaller files, which is preferable if you need to distribute them on the Internet.

However, it must be noted that at the present time, only GNU versions of **diff** and **patch** are able to process this format. Consequently, although this format can be used to do a specific job, if you want to distribute a corrective file as broadly as possible, independently of different versions of **diff** and **patch**, it is preferable to use the more commonly recognized **-c** option.

(kernel version 2.0 à 2.2)

The unified output format is created using the **-u** option. Here is an example of this format:

```
$ diff -u patch2.2 patch2.3
--- patch2.2    Mon Mar  1 11:38:59 1999
+++ patch2.3    Mon Mar  1 11:39:05 1999
@@ -1,4 +1,4 @@
+supplement
 affidate
-bin.aa. aa
+bin.aa.     aa
 bin.aa.old
-extra line (2.2)
```

As with the **-c** option, a header appears with the names of the files and their last modification times. Below this header, the differences are indicated as follows:

Lines with the format @@ **-L1,NL1 +L2,NL2** @@ introduce a group of modifications to be applied to the files. These modifications are to be applied to **NL1** lines of the first file starting from line **L1**, so that they will be identical to the **NL2** lines of the second file starting from line **L2**.
- Each line beginning with a space is common to both files and must remain unchanged. Their presence provides references for the utility should it meet problems (the utility tolerates slight dissimilarities in lines encountered, but as soon as these dissimilarities become too great it re-synchronizes the modifications using the context lines).
- Lines prefixed with a + sign are present in the second file and absent in the first.
- Lines prefixed with a - sign are present in the first file and absent in the second.

We will now see how to apply these modifications using the **patch** utility.

➔ patch

The **patch** and **diff** utilities form a complementary pair for distributing new versions of the Linux kernel. This is very important as the Linux development teams are very active, often releasing kernel patches which are generally a mixture of corrections and improvements. Also, as the source of the Linux kernel 2.2.2 current version of February 1999 occupies over 71 megabytes of disk space, it is often out of the question to download the complete set of source files, or even to download only those files having changed. The technique used is to download only modification files, to be applied generally to the complete set of source files, which consequently need be installed only once.

Suppose that the current Linux kernel version is 2.2.1. The development team will have the complete file hierarchy for this version, in addition to the new file hierarchy for version 2.2.2, which has not yet been released. To prepare a new distribution that will not overload the network, the development team will create a patch as follows:

```
$ diff -ur linux-2.2.1 linux-2.2.2 > patch-2.2.2
$ gzip patch_2.2.2
```

The second command reduces the size of the file by compressing it (again to minimize download time).

It must be noted that the patch was created using the **-u** option, which results in a smaller file than the **-c** option would have produced. In any case, the **patch** command can detect the format used to create the **patch** file.

This utility functions as follows:

The command **patch** PATCH_FILE determines the file to which the modifications must be applied. When it has identified this file (patch2.2 in the example below) it renames it by adding a **.orig** extension and then applies the transformation.

(kernel version 2.0 à 2.2)

```
$ diff -u patch2.2 patch2.3 > patch2
$ cat patch2
--- patch2.2      Mon Mar  1 15:12:07 1999
+++ patch2.3      Mon Mar  1 15:13:34 1999
@@ -1,4 +1,4 @@
+supplement
 affidate
-bin.aa. aa
+bin.aa.       aa
 bin.aa.old
-extra line (2.2)
$ patch <patch2
Hmm...  Looks like a unified diff to me...
The text leading up to this was:
--------------------------
|--- patch2.2      Mon Mar  1 15:12:07 1999
|+++ patch2.3      Mon Mar  1 15:13:34 1999
--------------------------
Patching file patch2.2 using Plan A...
Hunk #1 succeeded at 1.
done
$ ls -l patch*
-rw-------   1 system    users        170 Mar  1 15:14 patch2
-rw-------   1 system    users         45 Mar  1 15:15 patch2.2
-rw-------   1 system    users         47 Mar  1 15:12 patch2.2.or
ig
-rw-------   1 system    users         45 Mar  1 15:13 patch2.3
$ diff -s patch2.2 patch2.3
Files patch2.2 and patch2.3 are identical
```

When the patch has been created, it is applied directly. The **patch** command determines the format (unified in this case) and applies the transformation. This process produces the file patch2.2.orig (the version of the patch2.2 file before modification) and a new patch2.2 file, which is now identical to the patch2.3 file.

The patch2.2 file was chosen for modification by **patch** for several reasons:
− because its name was present in the patch file
− because it will support the modifications contained in the patch.

```
$ diff -u patch2.2 patch2.3 > patch
$ rm patch2.3
rm: remove 'patch2.3'? y
$ mv patch2.2 patch2.3
```

```
$ patch <patch
Hmm...  Looks like a unified diff to me...
The text leading up to this was:
--------------------------
|--- patch2.2   Mon Mar   1 15:49:31 1999
|+++ patch2.3   Mon Mar   1 15:13:34 1999
--------------------------
Patching file patch2.3 using Plan A...
Hunk #1 succeeded at 1.
done
$ ls -l patch*
-rw-------   1 system   users      170 Mar   1 15:50
patch
-rw-------   1 system   users       45 Mar   1 15:50
patch2.3
-rw-------   1 system   users       47 Mar   1 15:49
patch2.3.orig
```

The above example illustrates these criteria: even renaming the first file as the second does not prevent patch from identifying it as the one to be modified.

On the other hand, if only one of the two files exists, and that file is able to support only the *reverse* transformation, patch notices this and requests confirmation before reversing the modification (thus restoring the file to its original state). In the following example, patch2.3 is the second file used to create the patch. The first file has been deleted:

```
$ patch <patch
Hmm...  Looks like a unified diff to me...
The text leading up to this was:
--------------------------
|--- patch2.2   Mon Mar   1 15:49:31 1999
|+++ patch2.3   Mon Mar   1 15:13:34 1999
--------------------------
Patching file patch2.3 using Plan A...
Reversed (or previously applied) patch detected!
  Assume -R? [y]
Hunk #1 succeeded at 1.
done
```

However, if **patch** can find neither of the two files, it requests, the name of the file to be patched:

```
$ rm -i patch2.3
rm: remove 'patch2.3'? y
$ patch <patch
Hmm...  Looks like a unified diff to me...
The text leading up to this was:
--------------------------
|--- patch2.2    Mon Mar  1 15:49:31 1999
|+++ patch2.3    Mon Mar  1 15:13:34 1999
--------------------------
File to patch:
```

If the **patch** command is unable to apply all or a part of the modifications, it creates a file with a **.rej** extension containing the modifications it could not apply.

```
$ patch <patch
Hmm...  Looks like a unified diff to me...
The text leading up to this was:
--------------------------
|--- patch2.2    Mon Mar  1 15:49:31 1999
|+++ patch2.3    Mon Mar  1 15:13:34 1999
--------------------------
Patching file patch2.3 using Plan A...
Hunk #1 failed at 1.
1 out of 1 hunks failed--saving rejects to patch
2.3.rej
done
$ cat patch2.3.rej
***************
*** 1,4 ****
  affidate
- bin.aa. aa
  bin.aa.old
- extra line (2.2)
--- 1,4 ----
+ supplement
  affidate
+ bin.aa.     aa
  bin.aa.old
```

Before using a file that was modified using this process, it is advisable to check that a file with a **.rej** extension was not created. For example, use the following command:

```
$ find . -type f -name "*.rej" -print
```

➜ uniq

uniq deletes consecutive duplicate lines from a file (provided that it has been sorted previously).

This command offers the following options:

- **-c** prefixes each line with the number of its occurrences in the input file.
- **-d** to output only lines that were duplicated in the input file
- **-u** to output only lines that were unique in the input file
- **-s** n so that **uniq** will skip over the leading **n** characters of each line when checking it to be unique
- **-f** n so that uniq will skip over the leading **n** fields of each line when checking whether or not it is unique. Fields are defined as strings separated by at least one space or tab character.

```
$ cat exo1
town a
town a
town b
town c
town d
town d
town e
town f
town f
town f
town g
town h
town h
```

(kernel version 2.0 à 2.2)

Chapter 14

```
town h
town h
$ uniq exo1
town a
town b
town c
town d
town e
town f
town g
town h
$ uniq -c exo1
      2 town a
      1 town b
      1 town c
      2 town d
      1 town e
      3 town f
      1 town g
      4 town h
$ uniq -d exo1
town a
town d
town f
town h
$ uniq -u exo1
town b
town c
town e
town g
$ cat uniq.txt
Portsmouth   Hampshire
Winchester   Hampshire
Bournemouth  Dorset
Poole   Dorset
Brighton   Sussex
Eastbourne   Sussex
Hastings   Sussex
Newhaven   Sussex
Dover   Kent
$ uniq -f1 -c uniq.txt
      2 Portsmouth   Hampshire
      2 Bournemouth  Dorset
      4 Brighton   Sussex
      1 Dover   Kent
```

Using Linux

The last command shows the number of consecutive occurrences of the second field. First field occurrences were not taken into account in the calculation as this was not asked. However, as **uniq** displays whole lines, they appear in the result, but should be ignored in this context.

→ **tr**

This command carries out certain actions on characters read on its standard input before transmitting them to its output, hence the name **tr** for translate. The following actions are possible:
− replacement
− deletion
− deletion of repeated characters

The third action above can be combined with the first two.

To specify the first of these actions, the following syntax is used:

`tr string1 sting2`

It must be noted that, unlike the other commands, **tr** cannot read a file other than one redirected to its input. Consequently, redirected inputs and pipes are used when working with this command. In addition, the result will be displayed on the standard output, which must be redirected if you want to keep a record of it.

Each character read from its standard input and contained in **string1**, will be replaced by the character *in the corresponding position* in **string2**.

(kernel version 2.0 à 2.2)

The two lists normally have the same length, but what happens if they do not? If **string2** is longer than **string1** the extra characters are ignored. Conversely, if **string1** is longer than **string2** the result will depend on the system being used:

1. The POSIX.2 standard does not define the result
2. With a BSD system the last character of **string2** is repeated until this list is as long as **string1**
3. System V truncates **string1** to the same length as **string2**

By default, the Linux **tr** command, coming from the GNU environment, behaves like the BSD version. You can obtain a System V result by using **-t**.

Each list can be specified exhaustively or using intervals as for the shell. In addition, you can use the following notations:
− [c*n] in **string2** expands to **n** times the character **c**
− [c*] in **string2** expands to as many times the character **c** as necessary to make **string2** the same length as **string1**
− [:character-class:] allows you to specify one of the following character-classes:
   alnum   for letters and digits
   alpha   for letters
   blank   for horizontal whitespace
   cntrl   for control characters
   graph   for printable characters excluding spaces
   lower   for lowercase letters
   print   for printable characters including spaces
   punct   for punctuation characters
   space   for horizontal and vertical whitespaces
   upper   for uppercase letters
   xdigit for hexadecimal digits

In addition, if **string1** is too long or too complicated, it might be preferable to specify it by defining all the characters that are *not* in it. This can be done using the **-c** (complement) option which indicates that **string1** must contain all possible characters except those specified.

One example of the use of **tr** is to transform uppercase to lowercase and vice versa:

```
$ cat join1
Euston     Northern
Queensway  Central
Knightsbridge  Piccadilly
Bayswater  District
Blackfriars  Circle
Aldgate    Metropolitan
$ tr a-z A-Z <join1
EUSTON     NORTHERN
QUEENSWAY  CENTRAL
KNIGHTSBRIDGE  PICCADILLY
BAYSWATER  DISTRICT
BLACKFRIARS  CIRCLE
ALDGATE    METROPOLITAN
```

Here is another example:

```
$ cat sort1
Robert       Preston     442    66.10.26
Damien       Reading     355    72.09.12
Leonard      Salisbury   670    70.12.03
Leonard      Salisbury   670    72.05.14
Lara         Brighton    339    67.04.01
Gina         Aldershot   167    64.08.30
Gerard       Salisbury   670    70.05.01
$ cat sort1 | tr " ." "./"
Robert......Preston...442...66/10/26
Damien......Reading...355...72/09/12
Leonard...Salisbury...670...70/12/03
Leonard...Salisbury...670...72/05/14
Lara.......Brighton...339...67/04/01
Gina......Aldershot...167...64/08/30
Gerard....Salisbury...670...70/05/01
```

To delete characters, **tr** uses the following syntax:

```
tr -d string
```

(kernel version 2.0 à 2.2)

In this case, all characters read on the standard input and appearing in **string**, will be deleted:

```
$ cat tr.txt
1:city a
2:city a
3:city b
4:city c
5:city d
6:city d
7:city e
8:city f
9:city f
10:city f
11:city g
12:city h
13:city h
14:city h
15:city h
$ tr -d 0-9 < tr.txt
city a
city a
city b
city c
city d
city d
city e
city f
city f
city f
city g
city h
city h
city h
city h
```

One useful application of **tr** is the deletion of the "carriage-return" character present in MS-DOS files. Before reading these files on Unix, you must first get rid of this character. **tr** is very convenient to use for this operation as long as you know that the ASCII code for "carriage-return" is "\015". Here is the command to use:

```
tr -d "\015" <DOS.FILE  >UNIX.FILE
```

A certain number of control characters can be transformed, provided you know how to specify them. For these, backslash (\) escape sequences are used. Here is a list of supported sequences:

\a	alarm bell (Ctrl G)
\b	back-space (Ctrl H)
\f	form-feed (Ctrl L)
\n	new line (Ctrl J)
\r	carriage return (Ctrl M)
\t	horizontal tab (Ctrl I)
\v	vertical tab (Ctrl K)
\\	backslash character (\)

If you require another character not in this list you can specify its ASCII code in octal (1 to 3 digits), also prefixed with a backslash (\).

To delete consecutive character repetitions, use the following syntax:

```
tr -s string
```

Thus, if a character present in **string** appears several times consecutively on the standard input, **tr** deletes repeated occurrences of the character so as to leave only one occurrence on the output.

This function is often combined with the **cut** command. Suppose you want to produce a list of all the **ttys** currently being used. You can use the **who** command and extract the second field from its output. However, the fields are separated by several spaces and it is inconvenient to count them so as to get the tty field position (this is not the second field for the **cut** command precisely because there are several spaces before it). Instead of counting spaces, you can delete all repeated spaces and then ask **cut** to extract the second field.

(kernel version 2.0 à 2.2)

Chapter 14

```
$ who
system     ttyp0      Feb 10 09:12 (:0.0)
root       ttyp1      Feb 12 23:49 (:0.0)
webroot    ttyp3      Feb 13 16:34 (arthur.dorset.)
charlie    ttyp4      Feb 13 16:38 (:0.0)
$ who|tr -s " "| cut -d " " -f2
ttyp0
ttyp1
ttyp3
ttyp4
```

The **-s** option can be combined with the other two actions (replacement and deletion). In all cases, the **-s** option will be applied after the other action.

```
$ cat exo1
I am going
to the seaside
today
$ cat exo1 | tr -cs [:alnum:] "\n"
I
am
going
to
the
seaside
today
```

The above command reads all input lines and transforms them into output lines with one word on each.

Combining the **-d** and **-s** options requires a special approach. For this you must specify two lists: the first list containing the characters you want to delete, and the second list containing the characters for which you want to delete consecutive repetitions.

➔ **expand**

This filter converts tabs into spaces. By default, each tab is replaced by as many spaces as necessary to correspond to tabs positioned 8 spaces apart. To modify this default value, use the **-n** option, where **n** is the number of spaces between tab positions.

The **-i** option replaces only tabs that appear at the beginning of lines.

```
$ cat expand.txt
         city      a
         city      a
         city      b
         city      c
         city      d
         city      d
         city      e
         city      f
         city      f
         city      f
         city      g
         city      h
         city      h
         city      h
         city      h
$ expand -4 expand.txt
    city      a
    city      a
    city      b
    city      c
    city      d
    city      d
    city      e
    city      f
    city      f
    city      f
    city      g
    city      h
    city      h
    city      h
    city      h
$ expand -i -4 expand.txt
    city         a
    city         a
    city         b
    city         c
    city         d
    city         d
    city         e
    city         f
    city         f
```

(kernel version 2.0 à 2.2)

```
    city        f
    city        g
    city        h
    city        h
    city        h
    city        h
```

➜ **unexpand**

This command, the opposite of **expand**, converts spaces to tabs. By default, it converts 8 consecutive spaces into a tab, and only at the beginning of lines. This default functionality can be modified using the following options:

- **-n** indicates the number of consecutive spaces to be replaced by a tab
- **-a** also replaces spaces which are not at the beginning of lines

```
$ cat unexpand.txt
    city        a
    city        a
    city        b
    city        c
    city        d
    city        d
    city        e
    city        f
    city        f
    city        f
$ unexpand -4 unexpand.txt
        city        a
        city        a
        city        b
        city        c
        city        d
        city        d
        city        e
        city        f
        city        f
        city        f
```

➔ fold

This command wraps input lines by adding a newline so that they do not exceed a specified width. The line width by default is 80 columns, which may be modified using the **-w** option. The number of columns is not necessarily the same as the number of characters, as tab characters generally occupy several columns. **fold** is able to detect this.

The **fold** command offers the following options:

- **-w** indicates the number of columns
- **-s** folds lines at word boundaries. The line is folded at the last white space (if any) that falls within the maximum line width.

```
$ fold -w 40 fold.txt
This command inserts a newline in each l
ine as soon as the line width reaches 80
columns. This default value can be modif
ied using the -w option.
$ fold -w 40 -s fold.txt
This command inserts a newline in each
line as soon as the line width reaches
80 columns. This default value can be
modified using the -w option.
```

➔ fmt

The **fmt** command is the opposite of **fold**. It joins lines together to produce output lines of up to 75 characters (by default). This value can be modified using the **-w** option. In addition, this line preserves empty lines, spacing between words and indentation (lines with differing indentation are not joined together).

```
$ cat fmt.txt
This command joins together lines so that

the output lines

will be up to
 75 columns,
 a default     value you can
  modify using the -w option.
$ fmt fmt.txt
This command joins together lines so that

the output lines

will be up to
 75 columns, a default     value you can
  modify using the -w option.
```

Here are two of the options offered by fmt:

> **-u** reduces the spacing between words to a minimum
>
> **-p** the character following the **-p** option indicates that only lines prefixed by this character (and possibly preceded by white space) must be processed.

```
$ fmt -u fmt.txt
This command joins together lines so that

the output lines

will be up to
 75 columns, a default value you can
  modify using the -w option.
```

➔ **rev**

The **rev** command reads from its standard input or from files passed as arguments, and reproduces the lines on its standard output, reversing the order of the characters on each line.

```
$ cat join1
Euston    Northern
Queensway    Central
Knightsbridge    Piccadilly
Bayswater    District
Blackfriars    Circle
Aldgate    Metropolitan

$ rev join1
nrehtroN    notsuE
lartneC    yawsneeuQ
yllidacciP    egdirbsthginK
tcirtsiD    retawsyaB
elcriC    srairfkcalB
natiloporteM    etagdlA
```

B. Time Management

A set of commands is available to provide you with time related information. Here is a selection of them:
- **date** displays the date, time, time zone and current year. You can opt to display this information selectively. The same command allows the Administrator to modify these system parameters.
- **cal** displays a simple calendar, the current month by default. You can also display a calendar for a specific month or year.
- **time** allows you to display the execution time for a command: the time elapsed since it was started and the CPU usage time in user and kernel modes
- **times** is a bash built-in command showing cumulated user and system times for the current shell and all its child processes which have terminated.
- **at** to specify commands to be executed later.
- **crontab** to adjust the settings for the cyclic execution of a command

(kernel version 2.0 à 2.2)

➔ **date**

By default, this command displays the date, time, time zone and current year. You can also select which information you wish to display using the following, unusual, syntax:

`date "+FORMAT"`

The +FORMAT argument is a character string specifying what **date** must display. This string can be composed of format directives and ordinary text to be displayed as it is. Format directives are escape sequences introduced by a % character, indicating specific actions.

Here are the directives available:
- %A   full weekday name
- %a   abbreviated weekday name
- %B   full month name
- %b   abbreviated month name
- %c   date, time, time zone and year
- %d   day of the month (01 to 31)
- %D   date in mm/dd/yy format
- %H   hour (00 to 23)
- %I   hour (01 to 12) (%uppercase i)
- %j   day of the year (001 to 366)
- %k   hour (0 to 23) (Linux addition)
- %l   hour (01 to 12) (Linux addition) (%lowercase L)
- %m   month (01 to 12)
- %M   minute (00 to 59)
- %p   AM or PM
- %r   time, 12-hour format (hh:mm:ss AM or PM)
- %s   number of seconds since 00:00:00 on 1 January 1970 (Linux addition)
- %S   seconds (00 to 59)
- %T   time, 24-hour format (hh:mm:ss)
- %U   week number (00 to 53), taking Sunday as the first day of the week

%w	day of the week (0 to 6), taking Sunday as 0
%W	week number (00 to 53), taking Monday as the first day of the week
%X	time in default format according to selected language
%x	date in mm/dd/yy format
%Y	year in four digits
%y	year in two digits
%Z	time zone

In addition to these date and time directives, the following general formatting directives are also available:

%%	to display the % character
%n	inserts a newline
%t	inserts a horizontal tab

Here are a few examples of this command:

```
[9]-system(merlin)~:date
Mon Feb  8 15:32:15 MET 1999
[10]-system(merlin)~:date +Hello
Hello
[11]-system(merlin)~:date "+Hello%nToday : %A %d %B
%Y%nWeek   : %W"
Hello
Today : Monday 08 February 1999
Week  : 06
[12]-system(merlin)~:date "+Hello%nToday%t%A %d %B
%Y%nWeek%t%W"
Hello
Today   Monday 08 February 1999
Week    06
```

Looking beyond its apparent complexity, this command has many varied applications: for example, to create a file with the date as its name extension:

```
[13]-system(merlin)~:touch today.$(date +%m%d%y)
[14]-system(merlin)~:ls -l tod*
-rw-------   1 system   users        855 Feb  8 15:40 today.020899
```

→ **cal**

By default, this utility displays the calendar of the current month. If you specify one number argument, **cal** displays the calendar for the year corresponding to this number. If you specify two number arguments, **cal** displays the calendar for the month corresponding to the first argument, of the year (on 4 digits) corresponding to the second argument.

Here are two examples:

```
[24]-system(merlin)~:cal
     February 1999
Su Mo Tu We Th Fr Sa
    1  2  3  4  5  6
 7  8  9 10 11 12 13
14 15 16 17 18 19 20
21 22 23 24 25 26 27
28
[25]-system(merlin)~:cal 04 2002
     April 2002
Su Mo Tu We Th Fr Sa
    1  2  3  4  5  6
 7  8  9 10 11 12 13
14 15 16 17 18 19 20
21 22 23 24 25 26 27
28 29 30
```

→ **time**

The **time** command displays the execution time of the script, command or program specified as an argument. The following times are displayed:
- real time: the time elapsed since the start of the execution
- user time: the time used by the process in user mode, i.e. the time taken to execute the program's own code, not including any system calls it may have made.
- system time: CPU time used for the execution of system calls required by the program.

```
[merlin]# time find / -name "passwd*"
/var/man/cat1/passwd.1.gz
/usr/bin/passwd
/usr/man/man1/passwd.1
/usr/man/man5/passwd.5.gz
/usr/man/man5/passwd.5
/home/ftp/etc/passwd
/home/system/cops_104/passwd.chk
/home/system/cops_104/docs/passwd.chk
/home/system/cops_104/perl/passwd.chk
/home/system/cops_104/passwd.chk.old
/etc/passwd
/etc/passwd.OLD
/etc/passwd-
Command had non-zero exit status 1
0.88user
4.42system
1:56.56elapsed
```

The profile of the **time** output gives useful information on the real usage of the CPU by the command passed as an argument. The greater the ratio between user time and system time, the less the CPU was required by the command.

A high system load may have several causes. An obvious one is where the CPU has to share its activity between a multitude of processes. However, this is not the case in the above example where the system loading was caused more by heavy disk accessing rather than by any real loading of the CPU. Consequently, results should be interpreted with care.

➔ **times**

This is a shell built-in command displaying cumulated user and system times: for the current shell, on the first line, and for its child processes, on the second line.

Here is an example of this command:

```
[34]-system(merlin)~:times
0m0.19s 0m0.22s
0m1.15s 0m2.84s
```

(kernel version 2.0 à 2.2)

Chapter 14

Concerning time management, in common with all Unix systems, Linux is able to execute commands either at a later time or cyclically. These two sub-systems use the following commands:

at manages jobs for later execution

crontab adjusts settings for cyclic execution

It must be noted that standard Unix in general, and Linux in particular, do not implement real batch processing that operates at off-peak times.

➔ **at**

The **at** command executes a command at a given time. Here is the general syntax of this command:

at [options] TIME

You can specify the TIME argument in several ways. You can indicate the required time in a hhmm or hh:mm, 24-hour format. If the indicated time is already past, the command(s) concerned will be executed the following day at the specified time. You can also indicate the time in 12-hour format with an AM or PM suffix. The following specifications are also accepted:

midnight for 00:00

noon for 12:00

teatime for 16:00

In addition to the time, you can add a date in either absolute or relative format.

The absolute format can be one of the following:

MMDDYY with month, day and year, each indicated with two digits

MM/DD/YY same format but with a / separator.

MM.DD.YY same format but with a . separator.

The relative format is indicated using a number followed by the name of the units involved (minutes, hours or days).

One usage of a relative time is to indicate that you want a command to be executed in, say, 4 hours from the current time. In this case, you can use the very useful **now** keyword to give the following command:

```
at now + 4 hours
```

> *In some distributions, the execution sub-system depends on the **atrun** process which is executed cyclically by the **cron** process (**cron** is described later on in this chapter). By default, **atrun** is started every 5 minutes. As a result, the precision of the **at** command is also 5 minutes. This is generally sufficient and avoids overloading the system unnecessarily, especially if there are not very many **at** calls. Users must be aware of this mechanism though, otherwise they may be dismayed not to see their jobs executed at the exact time they specified.*

In recent versions, the delayed-execution mechanism is dissociated from the cyclic mechanism and uses the independent **atd** process. **atd** provides a starting-time precision of one minute.

When you have specified when you want the execution to take place, you must then specify which commands you want to execute. By default, the **at** command waits for you to enter these commands on the standard input. However, it is often more convenient to group them together in a file and send the contents to **at** through a pipe:

```
$ cat cmd.at
echo -n "Today's date is :"
date
$ cat cmd.at | at 1012
Job 7 will be executed using /bin/sh
```

(kernel version 2.0 à 2.2)

Chapter 14

Instead of sending the file contents via the standard input, you can request **at** to read the file explicitly, using the **-f** option.

```
$ at -f cmd.at 1012
Job 12 will be executed using /bin/sh
```

at indicates that the request has been submitted by displaying its job number. In addition, it is specified that the commands will be executed using the *Bourne-shell* (or more precisely, an emulation of the *Bourne-shell*). Consequently, syntax elements specific to the *C-shell* or the *Korn-shell*, should be avoided. If this is not practical, you must call the appropriate shell explicitly, in the command line submitted to **at**.

When the command has been executed, the result is returned to you by e-mail (as there is no guarantee that you will be connected when the commands are executed). Moreover, e-mail is the best way for the system to send the result and certainly better than transmitting the command output to your login terminal.

If the command produces no output, no mail is sent (unless you use the -**m** option so as to be informed of the command execution in all circumstances).

Other options are available that will be presented with the **atq** and **atrm** commands.

Some users may not be allowed to use the **at** command. This is because before doing anything else, **at** checks to see if the user is included in the /etc/at.deny file, in which case it refuses its services. The only solution to this problem is to discuss the matter with your system administrator.

➔ atq

The **atq** command lists jobs that are awaiting execution after having been submitted:

```
$ atq
Date                    Owner    Queue    Job#
10:12:00 02/23/99       soloa    c        14
10:12:00 02/23/99       soloa    c        15
```

In reality, **atq** is a link to the **at -l** command.

In common with **lpq**, this command is often used to obtain the numbers of jobs you want to cancel (using the **atrm** command).

➔ atrm

In common with **atq**, **atrm** is a link to the **at** command, this time in its form **at -d**.

In contrast to **lprm** (which deletes the last submission by default), you must indicate one or more job numbers when you call this command. In addition, **atrm** stays silent.

➔ cron

cron, named after Chronos, the greek god of time, is not a command. It is the process that manages the execution of scheduled commands. In some distributions, this process may be called **crond**. On Linux, its role is to search the file containing the cyclic command execution parameters, for each authorized user. These files are generally located in the **/var/spool/cron/crontabs** directory (although they may be located elsewhere). As general users do not have access permission, they must use the special command provided for editing these files. This command is called **crontab**.

(kernel version 2.0 à 2.2)

➔ **crontab**

The **crontab** command defines the execution frequency of commands that users wish to execute cyclically. More generally, this command maintains the crontab file containing execution parameters used by **cron**, by editing, listing or deleting its contents.

To this end, you should edit or create a file named the same as your user name, situated in the base directory of the **cron** sub-system.

This file is edited using the **crontab -e** command.

It must be noted that the default editor is either **vi** or that indicated in the VISUAL variable (if defined).

Empty lines are ignored as are those starting with a # character (the # character identifies comment lines). Active lines must be composed of six fields separated with spaces.

As both of the **cron** variations are implemented on Linux, we will present only their common characteristics. The Linux on-line help pages provide details of each of these variations.

The first five fields define the execution frequency of the command, which is contained in the sixth field. The contents of these five fields are as follows:

Field 1 indicates the minutes, from 0 to 59

Field 2 indicates the hour, from 0 to 23

Field 3 indicates the day of the month, from 1 to 31

Field 4 indicates the month, from 1 to 12

Field 5 indicates the day of the week, from 0 to 6, starting from Sunday.

You can define each of these fields in several ways:
- by indicating a value
- by indicating an exhaustive list of values separated by commas (,)
- by indicating a range, separating the first and last values by a dash (-)
- by combining the above two methods
- by indicating all possible values using the asterisk (*) character.

Here are some examples:

0 7 * * 1-5 cmd
The **cmd** command is executed every morning et seven o'clock, from Monday to Friday.

0,15,30,45 * * * * cmd
The command is executed every 15 minutes every day in the year.

***/15 * * * * cmd**
Many versions offer this more convenient syntax to define an interval. This line is equivalent to the previous one.

0 */2 * 1-6,9-12 * cmd
The command will be executed every two hours every day from January to June, and from September to December.

0 0 1 * 1 cmd
The **cmd** command will be executed at midnight at the beginning of each month and every Monday. When the day of the month and the day of the week are defined, there is an implicit logical OR between these fields (execution will take place if the day is the day in the week, or the day in the month, or both).

(kernel version 2.0 à 2.2)

Once the file has been saved, the **crontab** command offers two other options to manage its contents:

> **-l** displays the contents of the crontab file
>
> **-d or -r** deletes the crontab file. **-d** is used by the Dillon version while **-r** is used by the VixieCron version. The latter convention conforms better with POSIX.

Rather than deleting a crontab file, it is advisable to convert its lines to comments. By doing this, you have only to delete the # character at the start of the line in order to reactivate it, instead of re-entering its contents.

Here is an example of the crontab file.

```
$ crontab -l
# This updates the database for 'locate'
every day:
40 07 * * *         updatedb 1 /dev/null 2 /dev/null
#
#
#
0 */2 * * * /usr/local/sbin/sulog.trim
0 */2 * * * /usr/local/sbin/auth.trim
# Nettoyage du fichier /var/account/pacct - 14/02/1999
0  0  * * * /root/scripts/clean_pacct
# Gestion des fichiers de log par newsyslog -
15/02/1999
0 */2 * * * /usr/sbin/newsyslog
```

As with **at**, the administrator can prevent some or all of the users from using the cyclic-command execution mechanism.

C. Message commands

In common with Unix, Linux has a number of utilities allowing you to communicate with other users on the same system or on other, interconnected, systems. These commands are as follows:

- **news** to read system user information messages
- **write** to send a message to another user, if the other user allows you to do so (see **mesg**)
- **wall** to send a message to all users allowing you to do so
- **mesg** to allow or disallow messages being sent to you with **write** or **wall**
- **mail** for mail management
- **biff** to choose to be notified or not when mail arrives
- **talk** to communicate with another user interactively, whether you are connected on the same system or not

➔ **news**

Not to be confused with the Internet news, Linux news is a utility which allows the system administrator to communicate with other system users by means of news items. These news items are generally stored in files in the **/var/news** directory.

The **news** command allows users to read these internal news items. Each time you read these items, news updates the timestamp on the .news_time file in your home directory (this file is created automatically when you use **news** for the first time). By these means, news items which are earlier than this date will no longer be displayed (unless explicitly requested).

(kernel version 2.0 à 2.2)

By default, **news** displays all *current* items (i.e. those with dates later than the $HOME/.news_time timestamp).

```
$ news

** info.1 (root)   Tue Feb 16 19:25:47 1999

Nautical activities will be resumed next week-end.
```

This command offers the following options:

- **-a** to view all the items stored in /var/news.
- **-n** to view the names of current items (filenames from /var/news) without updating your **.news_time** timestamp.
- **-s** tells you how many current items there are.

```
$ news -s
news: 4 news articles
$ news -n
news: news.1 info.1 cine pay
$ news

** cine (root)   Tue Feb 16 19:32:52 1999

The film "the private life of a computer" will be showing
next Friday.
** pay (root)   Tue Feb 16 19:33:29 1999
Pay slips for February will be issued on 5th March.
$ news -a

** info.1 (root)   Tue Feb 16 19:25:47 1999

Nautical activities will be resumed next week-end.
```

```
** cine (root)   Tue Feb 16 19:32:52 199

The film "the private life of a computer" will be showing
next Friday.
** pay (root)   Tue Feb 16 19:33:29 1999

Pay slips for February will be issued on 5th March.
```

➔ write

This command allows you to send a message to another user. It has the following syntax:

```
write USER [TTYNAME]
```

You can provide the message to **write** in two ways:
- You can enter the message from your keyboard after having started **write**, which waits for your input. Press [Ctrl]**D** to send the message.

```
$ logname
sgbd
$ write soloa
Hi there
^D
$
```

- or, you can transmit your message to **write** through a pipe, in which case you can compose your message in a file in advance.

When the **write** command is executed, the target user is notified that a message has been sent to him/her:

```
$ logname
soloa
$
Message from sgbd@merlin on ttyp3 at 12:03 ...
```

The TTYNAME option allows you to specify the terminal to which you want to send your message. This is useful if the target user has several simultaneous connections.

(kernel version 2.0 à 2.2)

```
$ logname
soloa
$ who -Hu
USER       LINE       LOGIN-TIME      IDLE    FROM
system     ttyp0      Feb 18 17:48    00:21   (:0.0)
system     ttyp1      Feb 18 18:39    13:09   (:0.0)
system     ttyp2      Feb 18 23:08    00:24   (:0.0)
system     ttyp3      Feb 19 12:03    00:06   (arthur.dorset.)
soloa      ttyp4      Feb 19 12:03      .     (arthur.dorset.)
[4]-soloa(merlin) ~:write system
write: system is logged in more than once; writing to ttyp3
Where are you now?
```

If the target has several connections, by default the **write** command will choose the terminal with the shortest idle time (the contents of the IDLE field of the **write** command output).

```
$ who -Hu
USER       LINE       LOGIN-TIME      IDLE    FROM
system     ttyp0      Feb 18 17:48      .     (:0.0)
system     ttyp1      Feb 18 18:39    13:10   (:0.0)
system     ttyp2      Feb 18 23:08    00:25   (:0.0)
system     ttyp3      Feb 19 12:03    00:07   (arthur.dorset.)
soloa      ttyp4      Feb 19 12:03      .     (arthur.dorset.)
[10]-soloa(merlin) ~:write system
write: system is logged in more than once; writing to ttyp0
How are you doing ?
```

The **write** command cannot transmit messages in the following situations:
- the target has disallowed messages being sent to him/her.
- you have disallowed messages being sent to you, thereby preventing the target from replying.

```
$ write sgbd
write: sgbd has messages disabled
$ mesg n
$ mesg
is n
$ write sgbd
write: you have write permission turned off.
```

Such situations are managed using **mesg**, which we will cover after the **wall** command.

➔ wall

This command allows you to send messages to all users that are logged-in. By default, the message is read on the standard input. In contrast to **write**, **wall** can read directly from a file whose name is passed as an argument.

It must be noted that when **wall** is executed by root, all users will receive the message whether they have disallowed **write** access or not.

➔ mesg

This command has two functions:
— to indicate whether or not your terminal currently allows messages to be sent to it
— to allow or disallow write access to your terminal

To activate the first of these functions, simply call **mesg** without options.

```
$ mesg
is n
```

For the second function, indicate **y** to allow messages to be sent or **n** to disallow them.

```
$ mesg y
$ mesg
is y
$ mesg n
$ mesg
is n
```

In fact, allowing or disallowing messages being sent is equivalent to changing the **group** and **other** write permissions for the special file associated with your terminal:

(kernel version 2.0 à 2.2)

Chapter 14

```
$ tty
/dev/ttyp2
$ mesg
is n
$ ls -l /dev/ttyp2
crwx------   1 system   users 3,  2 Feb 16 19:45 /dev/ttyp2
$ mesg y
$ ls -l /dev/ttyp2
crwx-w--w-   1 system   users  3,   2 Feb 16 19:45 /dev/ttyp2
```

→ **mail**

mail is a mail processing system which allows users to exchange messages. **mail** is not limited to a single system, each recipient having an address allowing messages to be transmitted to them across the network. The address is made up of two parts, separated by the @ character. The first part indicates the user name and the second part represents the Internet address of the machine hosting the account.

For the moment, we will limit ourselves to the command which allows you to manage sent and received messages. This command can be called **mail**, **Mail** or **mailx**. This name may vary from one system to the next according to the command's origins, but generally each command name is linked to the other two:

```
$ which mail mailx Mail
/bin/mail
/bin/mailx
/bin/Mail
$ cd /bin
$ ls -l mail Mail mailx
lrwxrwxrwx 1 root    root    13 Sep 17  1997 Mail -> /usr/bin/Mail
lrwxrwxrwx 1 root    root    13 Sep 17  1997 mail -> /usr/bin/Mail
lrwxrwxrwx 1 root    root    13 Sep 17  1997 mailx -> /usr/bin/Mail
$ ls -l /usr/bin/Mail
-rwxr-xr-  1 root   bin          59420 Aug 16  1996 /usr/bin/Mail
```

When mail arrives for you, it is added to the end of the file bearing your username in the /var/spool/mail directory and stays there until you view it. When you have viewed it, its contents are moved to the $HOME/mbox file.

To check if you have new mail use the **mail** command without options:
- either you have no new mail and you see a message such as that in the example below:

```
$ mail
No mail for system
```

- or, you have new mail, in which case the command displays the headers of your mail and goes into interactive mode. This is indicated by the **&** prompt:

```
$ mail
Mail version 5.5 6/1/90.   Type ? for help.
"/root/mbox": 4 messages
> 1 system@merlin.dorset Thu Jul 16 10:14 1669/75744 "Daily accounting sum"
  2 root@merlin.dorset Tue Feb 16 10:11 25/847 "Quota usage on system"
  3 root@merlin.dorset Mon Feb 15 00:00 12/428 "cron: /root/scripts/c"
  4 root@merlin.dorset Tue Feb 16 00:00  12/428 "cron:/root/scripts/c"
&
```

In interactive mode, **mail** offers a set of sub-commands for which a short description can be viewed using the **help** or **?** sub-command:

```
& ?
      Mail    Commands
t <message list>          type messages
n                         goto and type next message
e <message list>          edit messages
f <message list>          give head lines of messages
d <message list>          delete messages
s <message list> file     append messages to file
u <message list>          undelete messages
R <message list>          reply to message senders
r <message list>          reply to message senders
and all recipients
pre <message list>        make messages go back to /
usr/spool/mail
m <user list>             mail to specific users
q                         quit, saving unresolved
messages in mbox
x                         quit, do not remove system
mailbox
h                         print out active message
headers
!                         shell escape
cd [directory]            chdir to directory or home
if none given
```

(kernel version 2.0 à 2.2)

```
A <message list> consists of integers, ranges of same,
or user names separated
by spaces. If omitted, Mail uses the last message
typed.

A <user list> consists of user names or aliases
separated by spaces.
Aliases are defined in .mailrc in your home directory.
```

➔ biff

You can decide how you want the system to let you know when new mail arrives:
— either by displaying the mail header and first few lines
— or by not notifying you at all, if you prefer to check for yourself periodically

The **biff** command allows you to check which option is active and/or to opt for the other option.

When called without arguments, **biff** returns **is y** if you would be notified when mail arrives, or **is n** if you would not.

Specify **y** to ask the system to notify you when mail arrives, or **n** to ask the system not to.

```
$ biff
is n
$ biff y
$ biff
is y
```

```
$ biff
is n
$ ls -l /dev/ttyp3
crw-------   1 system users 3, 3 Feb 19 17:13 /dev/ttyp3
$ biff y
$ ls -l /dev/ttyp3
crwx------   1 system users 3, 3 Feb 19 17:13 /dev/ttyp3
```

➔ talk

This command allows you to talk to another user in real-time. It has the following general syntax:

```
talk PERSON [TTYNAME]
```

The PERSON argument is the user's login name, if your correspondent is on the same system. Otherwise, it is your correspondents address (cf **mail** command).

Here is an example of the interactive screen that appears when you call **talk**.

```
[Waiting for your party to respond]



m------------------------------------------------j









Message from Talk_Daemon@merlin at 18:32 ...
talk: connection requested by system@merlin.dorset.uk.
talk: respond with:   talk system@merlin.dorset.uk
```

D. Compressing files

On Unix, there are a number of compression utilities

Originally, each of the two main Unix branches, BSD and System V, had its own compression and decompression commands:
— **pack/unpack** for System V
— **compact/uncompact** for BSD 4.2

However, two other open source utilities appeared, outperforming the classical Unix utilities. First **compress/uncompress** appeared and became the standard Unix compression utility because of its performance. Then came **gzip** which is the most widely used tool to compress Unix public domain files available on the Internet. The **gzip** utility has become the Linux standard compressor, even though **compress** is also available.

Recently, further improvements in compression ratios are offered by the **bzip2** utility.

➔ **compress**

This utility compresses specified files using the Lempel-Ziv algorithm. The original files are replaced by files with a .Z extension, preserving owner permissions, last access and last modification times as the following example shows:

```
[97]-system(merlin)~:ls -l bibli.slk
-rwx------   1 system   users     225672 Sep 27 16:12 bibli.slk*
98]-system(merlin)~:ls -lu bibli.slk
-rwx------   1 system   users     225672 Dec 19 14:51 bibli.slk*
[100]-system(merlin)~:compress bibli.slk
[101]-system(merlin)~:ls -l bibli.slk.Z
-rwx------   1 system   users      61869 Sep 27 16:12 bibli.slk.Z*
[102]-system(merlin)~:ls -lu bibli.slk.Z
-rwx------   1 system   users      61869 Dec 19 14:51 bibli.slk.Z*
```

It must be noted that if **compress** is executed by root, the group and other permissions are also preserved.

Several options are available:

- **-d** decompresses the file whose name is passed as an argument. The **uncompress** command is equivalent to **compress -d** and in some cases it is a simple physical or symbolic link to this command.

- **-c** sends the result to the output instead of a file. When used with the **-d** option or the **uncompress** command, it functions like the **zcat** command.

- **-v** displays percentage reduction

-**v** displays the version of the utility along with any preprocessor flags

The following examples illustrate these options:

```
[179]-system(merlin)~:ls -l bibli.slk
-rwx------   1 system   users     225672 Sep 27 16:12
bibli.slk*
[180]-system(merlin)~:compress -v bibli.slk
bibli.slk:  -- replaced with bibli.slk.Z Compression:
72.58%
[181]-system(merlin)~:compress -d bibli.slk.Z
[182]-system(merlin)~:ls -l bibli.slk.Z
-rwx------   1 system   users      61869 Sep 27 16:12
bibli.slk.Z*
[183]-system(merlin)~:compress -d bibli.slk.Z
[184]-system(merlin)~:ls -l bibli.slk
-rwx------   1 system   users     225672 Sep 27 16:12
bibli.slk*
[185]-system(merlin)~:compress -c bibli.slk tmp.Z
[186]-system(merlin)~:ls -l tmp.Z
-rw-------   1 system   users      61869 Jan 14 22:14
tmp.Z
```

As **compress** adds a 2-character extension to the file name, the latter must not exceed the maximum filename length minus 2. Maximum filename length depends on the file system used and is generally 255 characters.

➔ **gzip, gunzip**

gzip is the most widely used compression utility for a number of reasons:
— it is freely available
— it exists for a large number of systems
— it can decompress several compression formats
— it gives very good results, for both performance and compression ratio.

gzip uses the Lempel-Ziv algorithm LZ77. Specified files are replaced by compressed files of the same name plus the .gz extension.

(kernel version 2.0 à 2.2)

Chapter 14

```
$ ls -l ficres2
-rw------- 1 system   users    2364 Feb 27 12:11 ficres2
$ gzip ficres2
$ ls -l ficres2.gz
-rw------- 1 system   users     433 Feb 27 12:11 ficres2.gz
```

The size reduction in this example is 82.7%.

It must be noted that you can specify several files for processing by **gzip**. If no file is specified, **gzip** processes the bytes from its standard input which generally requires a redirection so as to save the result in a file.

If the filename is too long for the extension to be added it is truncated to suit (otherwise, for a 253-character filename for example, adding the extension would bring the size to 256 characters and thus exceed a 255 maximum). However, in all cases, the full original name is stored in the compressed image so that it can be correctly restored when decompressing.

In addition to its name, the last modification timestamp, the owner and the group are also written to the file. These will be restored identically, if the user carrying out the decompression is either root or the owner of the file.

Files are decompressed using the **gunzip** utility, which in reality is a link to **gzip -d**.

```
$ file /bin/gunzip
/bin/gunzip: symbolic link to gzip
```

It must be noted that files are always compressed, even if the resulting file is larger than the original (by 0.015 % maximum, allowing for the storage of management information).

gunzip can decompress files produced by **gzip**, **zip**, **compress** or **pack**, possessing .gz, -gz, .z, -z, .Z or -Z extensions. The file name must contain the extension but you do not need to specify it to **gunzip**. Also, **gunzip** will examine the file's magic number to determine its format (the magic number is also used by **file** to determine a file's type). In addition, before decompressing, **gunzip** verifies the integrity of the compressed file.

As gunzip works only which files with have appropriate extensions, it does not decompress indiscriminately as **compress** does. When decompressing, **gunzip** replaces the compressed file which the decompressed one unless you specifically request that it should preserve the compressed file. This can be done using the **-c** option that sends the decompressed result to the standard output (which you must redirect). Alternatively, you can use the **zcat** utility, which is presented in the next section.

gzip and **gunzip** offer numerous options. Here is a selection of those most widely used:

- **-c** the result is sent to the standard output, allowing the source file to be preserved intact. This applies to both compression, and decompression using **gunzip** or **gzip -d**.
- **-d** requests decompression rather than compression, which is the processing by default.
- **-l** Requests information on the file whose name is supplied as an argument. This information includes compressed and decompressed sizes, compression ratio and the decompressed name. When combined with the **-v** option, it also displays the **crc** value (allowing detection of any compression errors) and the timestamp (date and time) of the uncompressed file.

(kernel version 2.0 à 2.2)

```
$ gzip -l ficres2
compressed   uncompr. ratio uncompressed_name
      433       2364  82.7% ficres2
$ gzip -lv ficres2
method  crc      date  time    compressed   uncompr.
ratio uncompressed_name
defla 03a6929d Feb 27 12:11      433       2364
 82.7% ficres2
```

-N requests preservation of the original file name and timestamp (this is the default action when compressing; when decompressing, however, the restored name is normally that passed as an argument). When decompressing then, this option allows you to restore the name and timestamp stored in the compressed file, which you can view using the **-l** option.

Here is an example showing the functioning by defaut:

```
$ gzip ficres2
$ ls ficres3
/bin/ls: ficres3: No such file or directory
$ mv ficres2.gz ficres3.gz
$ gunzip ficres3
$ ls ficres3
ficres3
```

The **ficres2** file was compressed into the **ficres3** file. The decompression process results were also written to the **ficres3** file, by default.

The result would have been different with the **-N** option:

```
$ gzip ficres2
$ mv ficres2.gz ficres3.gz
$ gzip -l ficres3.gz
compressed  uncompr. ratio uncompressed_name
      433       2364  82.7% ficres3
$ gzip -lN ficres3.gz
compressed  uncompr. ratio uncompressed_name
      433       2364  82.7% ficres2
$ gzip -Nd ficres3.gz
$ ls ficres3
/bin/ls: ficres3: No such file or directory
$ ls ficres2
ficres2
```

- **-r** to compress/decompress the files in the directory supplied as an argument. This is done recursively.

- **-t** tests the integrity of the compressed file. It stays silent when the file is found to be correct.

- **-v** (verbose) displays name of compressed and decompressed files along with percentage reductions.

```
$ gzip -v ficres2
ficres2:                  82.9% -- replaced with
ficres2.gz
```

You can specify one of nine compression levels with **gzip**. These allow you to favor either compression speed or compression quality. Thus, **-1** optimizes compression speed and **-9** optimizes compression quality. By default compression level **-6** is used, which is biased towards compression quality.

Each time it is called, **gzip** checks the presence and contents of the **GZIP** environment variable. **GZIP** can contain **gzip** options. This means that you can avoid having to specify them explicitly each time you use this utility.

(kernel version 2.0 à 2.2)

Here is an example:

```
$ gzip ficres2
$ gunzip ficres2
$ export GZIP="-8 -v -N"
$ gzip ficres2
ficres2:                    82.9% -- replaced with
ficres2.gz
```

➔ zcat

zcat reads the contents of a file compressed using **pack**, **compress** or **gzip** and sends it to the standard output. The compressed file stays intact. As for **uncompress**, you do not have to indicate the .Z extension as this is assumed.

This command replaces the following pipeline:
`cat file.Z | compress -d`

➔ bzip2, bunzip2, bzcat

bzip2 is a new compress/decompress utility which is being used increasingly because it out-performs **gzip**, particularly on compression ratios. These performance improvements are due to the use of the Burrows-Wheeler algorithm.

In common with all compression utilities presented in this section, **bzip2** processes an uncompressed file and replaces it with the compressed result, which it renames by adding an extension (.bz2 in this case). Similarly, the last modification timestamp and permissions are preserved. **Owner** and **group** are also preserved when this utility is used by **root**.

One major drawback to the current version of **bzip2** is that it can decompress only those files it has compressed itself. In contrast, **gzip** can also work with files compressed using **pack** and **compress**.

When called without arguments, **bzip2** processes bytes read from its standard input and returns the result on its standard output, which you must redirect.

In common with **gzip**, **bzip2** is able to check for compression errors and corrupted files. The **bziprecover** utility attempts to restore damaged data.

Here are a few of the numerous **bzip2** options:

- **-c** sends the result of the compression or decompression to the standard output.
- **-d** requests decompression. The **bunzip2** command is a link to **bzip2 -d**. It must be noted that, unlike **compress** and **gzip**, it is essential to specify the extension of a file you want to decompress.

```
$ bzip2 -d BIBLI.slk
bzip2: Input file BIBLI.slk doesn't exist,
 skipping.
$ bzip2 -d BIBLI.slk.bz2
```

- **-f** forces overwriting of output files. This means that compression will be forced even if there is already a file having the same name as the uncompressed file with a **.bz2** extension.
- **-k** preserves input files when compressing or decompressing
- **-t** checks the integrity of files without decompressing them

```
$ bzip2 -t BIBLI.slk.bz2
$ bzip2 -tv BIBLI.slk.bz2
  BIBLI.slk.bz2: ok
```

(kernel version 2.0 à 2.2)

-v (verbose) shows the compression ratio for each compressed file. Indicating several **v**s increases the verbosity level but the extra information is not necessarily of any use to you without a sound knowledge of the algorithm used.

```
$ bzip2 -v BIBLI.slk
  BIBLI.slk:  6.793:1,  1.178 bits/byte, 85.28%
saved, 247090 in, 36374 out.
$ bzip2 -d BIBLI.slk.bz2
$ bzip2 -vv BIBLI.slk
  BIBLI.slk:
    block 1: crc = 0xe9af7795, combined CRC =
0xe9af7795, size = 247092
      final combined CRC = 0xe9af7795
      6.793:1,  1.178 bits/byte, 85.28% saved,
247090 in, 36374 out.
```

-1 ... -9 The higher the number (1 to 9) the better the compression ratio:

```
$ bzip2 -1 BIBLI.slk
$ ls -l BIBLI.slk.bz2
-rw-rw-r--   1 system   users
8449 Oct 31 09:25 BIBLI.slk.bz2
$ bzip2 -d BIBLI.slk.bz2
$ bzip2 -5 BIBLI.slk
$ ls -l BIBLI.slk.bz2
-rw-rw-r--   1 system   users
36374 Oct 31 09:25
BIBLI.slk.bz2
$ bzip2 -d BIBLI.slk.bz2
$ bzip2 -9 BIBLI.slk
$ ls -l BIBLI.slk.bz2
-rw-rw-r--   1 system   users
36374 Oct 31 09:25 BIBLI.slk.bz2
```

By default, compression level **-9** is used.

It must be noted that, although compression ratios are generally better with **bzip2** than with **gzip**, the latter utility is quicker overall. For example, to process the same file, **gzip** took 16.85 seconds for a default compression to 1 916 427 bytes, whereas **bzip2** needed 53.61 seconds to compress to 1 500 305 bytes. The choice of one or the other utility will depend on your needs, constraints and preferences.

The **bzcat** utility is a link to **bzip2 -dc**.

E. Process management

Before we discuss anything else, it will be useful to define a process. In contrast to an executable binary file, which is an inert object stored on a disk, a process is an active entity, requiring a certain number of resources: central memory, disk space and access, other processes...

Throughout its existence, a process has a number of states, varying from one system to another. Nevertheless, the *principal* states involved can be identified, as follows:

— **Ready** for execution or currently being executed.
   It might appear surprising that no distinction is made between these two concepts. This can be explained as follows:
   as soon as a process is ready for execution, it is included in the active processes table (task vector). Whether a process is running or not is only a question of the moment in time: the active processes share the CPU(s) in rapid rotation (this is the concept of context switching, indicated by the Linux **vmstat** and **procinfo** commands).

(kernel version 2.0 à 2.2)

- **Waiting**
  This means that the process is waiting for a resource or an event: for example, because it needs a resource currently being used by another process, or simply because it has made a request that has not yet been completed (end of input/output for instance).
- **Stopped**
  The process was stopped, usually after receiving a signal as a result of an external action, generally initiated by the user who started the process.
- **Zombie**
  This term might be surprising but it is well suited. This is a halted process which stays present in the active process table. It is what it sounds like, a "living-dead" process. It stays in this state as long as the process which created it does not receive its return status.

Like a user, a process has a unique identification in the system thanks to its PID (Process ID). In addition to a PID, a process has other characteristics, including the following:

RUID or Real UID	is the identity of the user who started the process
EUID or Effective UID	is the identity under which the process is running, which can be different from that of the user who started it. This is the case of a **setuid** program.
RGID or Real GID	is the group of the user who started the process
EGID or Effective GID	is the effective group to which the process belongs

The process **EUID** and **EGID** are used by the system to check access permissions.

Other characteristics and status values can be viewed using the **ps** (process status) command which, without options or arguments, lists your current processes:

```
$ ps
PID TTY STAT   TIME COMMAND
3887  p2  S    0:00 -bash
4525  p2  R    0:00 ps
```

By default, this list contains five columns:
− PID: discussed above
− TTY: the name of the special file managing the terminal to which the process is attached.
− STAT: the process state. This can be:
    R for ready (runnable),
    S for sleeping (interruptible waiting process),
    D for sleeping (uninterruptible waiting process),
    T for stopped (or traced) or
    Z for zombie.
− TIME: cumulated execution (CPU occupation) time
− COMMAND: the name of the process

The **ps** command offers a large number of options that will not be covered here as the most frequent usage of **ps** is to find out the **PID** of a process you want to stop.

Suppose that you want to stop a process called process1. To obtain its **PID**, you can use the following command:

```
$ ps | grep [p]rocess1
   4595  p2  S    0:00 sh process1
```

The square brackets are used to avoid the **grep** process appearing in the result. The same result could have been obtained with the following command:

```
ps | grep process1 | grep -v grep
```

(kernel version 2.0 à 2.2)

kill

Equipped with the PID of the process in question, you can now ask it to stop. This is done using the **kill** command, which allows you to send a request (called a signal) to a process. Most modern shells have a built-in **kill** when they support job management, covered in the next section. This built-in **kill** command has priority over any shell-external **kill** which may be present on the system.

There are approximately 30 signals managed by the system, but not all are at the user's disposal. To get a list of signals, use the **kill** command with the **-l** option.

```
kill  -l
 1) SIGHUP      2) SIGINT      3) SIGQUIT    4) SIGILL
 5) SIGTRAP     6) SIGIOT      7) SIGBUS     8) SIGFP
 9) SIGKILL    10) SIGUSR1    11) SIGSEGV   12) SIGUSR2
13) SIGPIPE    14) SIGALRM    15) SIGTERM   17) SIGCHLD
18) SIGCONT    19) SIGSTOP    20) SIGTSTP   21) SIGTTIN
22) SIGTTOU    23) SIGURG     24) SIGXCPU   25) SIGXFSZ
26) SIGVTALRM  27) SIGPROF    28) SIGWINCH  29) SIGIO
30) SIGPWR
```

In general, you will use only the following signals: SIGINT, SIGKILL, SIGSTOP and SIGCONT. Although you can send a signal by specifying its number, it is preferable to use its name. This is because the name is the same on all systems, while numbers may vary from one system version to another (it is rare but it can happen).

Here is the syntax of the **kill** command:

```
kill [-s signal] PID_LIST
```

By default, the SIGTERM signal will be sent. This is a termination request that the process(es) may or may not be able to handle. When they are programmed to process this signal, they carry out all actions necessary to terminate normally: closing open files, freeing memory, resetting the terminal. This is by far the most advisable method of stopping a process. However, some processes are not able to respond to this signal. In this case, you should try the SIGINT signal. If there is still no reaction, you must send the SIGKILL signal. This is a brutal death ordered by the kernel that no process can avoid, except for some rare exceptions such as an uninterruptible waiting process (D) or a zombie, which is already dead.

Apart from the system administrator, most users do not need to know the PID of processes they wish to stop, as, in most cases these will have been started in the background. For such processes, it is more practical to use **job** management techniques, where a **job** is a process that runs in the background.

Job management

Job management depends on the shell. It originated with the C-shell and was adopted by the Korn-shell and then by the Bash (Linux shell by default) Only the Bourne-shell does not support it.

When you execute a process in the background, you can continue to dialog with your terminal whilst your process is still running. To run a process in the background specify the **&** character at the end of the command line:

```
$ job1 &
[1] 8932
$
```

As soon as the command line has been checked, the process is started, and two pieces of information are displayed before the prompt reappears:
− the job number. In the example, this was the first job to have been started in the background

− the PID for the process

The **jobs** command lists the background processes (jobs):

```
$ jobs
[1]    Running                     job1 &
[2]    Running                     job3 &
[3]-   Running                     job4 &
[4]+   Running                     job2 &
```

It must be noted that **jobs** is a shell built-in command for the Korn-shell and the Linux bash.

By default, **jobs** provides three pieces of information:
− job number
− job status
− command line used to start the process

A plus sign (+) appears after the number of the most recent job, and a minus sign (-) appears after the number of the second-most recent job.

The **-l** option displays the PID numbers of the jobs, although this is not really needed to manage them:

```
$ jobs -l
[1]    8932 Running                 job1 &
[2]   10614 Running                 job3 &
[3]- 10624 Running                  job4 &
[4]+ 10633 Running                  job2 &
```

Unlike other processes, you can send a signal to a job very conveniently, without needing to know its PID.

There are several methods of indicating jobs to the shell built-in **kill** command, all of which are introduced using the % character. Here is the syntax involved:

```
kill [-signal] %process
```

Here are the different methods you can use to specify the process:

> **%n** to indicate the job number **n** (N.B. this is the job number as supplied by the **jobs** command. It is not its PID).
>
> **%%** to specify the last job started
>
> **%+** is equivalent to %%
>
> **%-** to specify the second-last job started
>
> **%string** to indicate the job for which the command line *starts* with the specified string. If this string is ambiguous, the command will fail (see example below).
>
> **%?string** to indicate the job for which the command line *contains* the specified string. Again, any ambiguity will cause the command to fail.

Here are some examples of these different methods of terminating a job with, notably, an illustration of an ambiguity problem in the fifth command:

```
$ jobs
[1]    Running                 job1 &
[2]    Running                 job3 &
[3]-   Running                 job4 &
[4]+   Running                 job2 &
$ kill %%
$ jobs
[1]    Running                 job1 &
[2]    Running                 job3 &
[3]-   Running                 job4 &
[4]+   Terminated              job2
$ jobs
[1]    Running                 job1 &
[2]-   Running                 job3 &
[3]+   Running                 job4 &
$ kill %job
kill: ambigious job spec: job
$ kill %job3
```

(kernel version 2.0 à 2.2)

```
$ jobs
[1]    Running                    job1 &
[2]-   Terminated                 job3
[3]+   Running                    job4 &
$ kill %?ob4
$ jobs
[1]-   Running                    job1 &
[3]+   Terminated                 job4
```

Converting a foreground process into a job

Suppose that you forget to enter the **&** character, and start a process in the foreground by mistake. As a result, you would not be able to work further on your terminal while this process was running. You can stop a foreground process by entering [Ctrl] C, but this may be dangerous if the process is dealing with files, as they can become incoherent, possibly rendering them unusable. There are two things you can do to solve this problem: either you wait for the process to finish, or you stop it so as to re-start it in the background.

To stop a foreground process, you cannot use the **kill** command, unless you have a multi-window system or access to another terminal. However, you can enter [Ctrl] Z which sends the SIGTSTP (*Terminal Stop*) signal to the process in the foreground. The process is stopped and it is placed in the background in this state.

Once it is in the background, you can re-start a process that was stopped by [Ctrl] Z by using the **bg** (background) shell built-in command. Called without arguments, this command restarts the last process that was stopped. Alternatively, you can indicate a specific job using one of the notations detailed above.

```
$ job1 &
[1] 15534
$ jobs
[1]+   Running                    job1 &
$ job2
```

```
[2]+    Stopped                 job2
$ jobs
[1]-    Running                 job1 &
[2]+    Stopped                 job2
$ bg
[2]+ job2 &
$ jobs
[1]-    Running                 job1 &
[2]+    Running                 job2 &
$ fg %-
job1
```

The **fg** (foreground) command does the inverse operation, bringing a job into the foreground (see example above). Again, using this command without an argument will bring the last job into the foreground.

stty command

This command can be useful when [Ctrl] C and [Ctrl] Z are not operational. Although these are the most commonly supported key combinations, some configurations or systems use different ones (this is the case for SCO UNIX for example). To find out the current settings for these and other functions use the **stty -a** command.

```
stty -a
speed 9600 baud; rows 24; columns 80; line = 0;
intr = ^C; quit = ^\; erase = ^H; kill = ^U; eof = ^D;
eol = <undef> eol2 = <undef> ; start = ^Q; stop = ^S;
susp = ^Z; rprnt = ^R; werase = ^W;
lnext = ^V; flush = ^O; min = 1; time = 0;
-parenb -parodd cs8 -hupcl -cstopb cread -clocal -crtscts
-ignbrk -brkint -ignpar -parmrk -inpck -istrip -inlcr -igncr icrnl
ixon -ixoff
-iuclc -ixany -imaxbe
opost -olcuc -ocrnl onlcr -onocr -onlret -ofill -ofdel
nl0 cr0 tab0 bs0 vt0 ff0
isig icanon iexten echo echoe echok -echonl -noflsh
-xcase -tostop -echoprt
echoctl echoke
```

(kernel version 2.0 à 2.2)

This command displays the current terminal settings, notably the key combinations associated with the SIGINT and SIGTSTP signals. The SIGINT signal is represented by the "intr" keyword. In the above example, it corresponds to "^C" which symbolises [Ctrl] C. The SIGTSTP signal is represented by "susp". In the above example, this corresponds to "^Z", symbolising [Ctrl] Z.

↓ personal notes ↓

Index

-, *33*
;, *34*
-, *180*
/bin, *18*
/boot, *18*
/dev, *18, 35*
/dev/null, *181*
/etc, *18*
/etc/group, *26 - 27*
/etc/issue, *30*
/etc/magic, *145*
/etc/man, *119*
/etc/motd, *31*
/etc/passwd, *25 - 27, 167*
/etc/profile, *94*
/home, *18*
/lib, *19*
/lost+found, *19*
/mnt, *19*
/proc, *19*
/tmp, *19, 56*
/usr, *19*
/usr/adm, *20*
/usr/bin/passwd, *54*
/usr/lib, *19*
/usr/local/lib, *21*
/usr/man, *118 - 119*
/var, *20*
/var/log, *20*
/var/news, *218*
/var/spool, *214*
:set all, *115*
<, *102*
&, *103*
>, *102, 104*
>>, *104*
\, *112, 128*
| |, *35*

A

Absolute path, *17*
Adding to end of file, *102*
adm, *19*
AIX, *122*
alias, *64 - 65, 87*
Alias management, *58*
Aliases, *63, 92*
allexport, *78*
ASCII, *77, 96, 159, 166, 199*
at, *206, 211 - 212*
AT&T, *8*
atd, *212*
atq, *214*
atrm, *214*
atrun, *212*
awk, *128 - 130*

B

Background, *243*
bash, *11, 31, 49, 58 - 59, 73, 75, 93 - 95, 240*
bg, *243*
bgnice, *78*
biff, *218, 225*
bin, *19*
Bourne-shell, *11, 31, 58, 75, 95, 98, 213, 240*
BSD, *11, 27, 44 - 45, 58, 122 - 123, 197, 226*
bunzip2, *233*
Burrows-Wheeler alogorithm, *233*
Byte stream, *98*
bzcat, *233*
bzip2, *227, 233*
bziprecover, *234*

C

C, *58*
C-shell, *11, 31, 58, 66, 73, 78, 95, 213, 240*
cal, *206, 209*
cat, *76, 152 - 154, 161*
cd, *17, 50, 80 - 82*
Central memory, *236*
chgrp, *28*
chmod, *45, 51*
cmd, *86*
cmp, *153, 179*
comm, *153, 180*
command, *62, 86 - 87*
Command history, *58, 66*
Command mode, *60*
compact, *226*
Comparing files, *179*
Compress, *227, 230, 233*
Compressing files, *226*
Compression ratio, *228, 233*
Conditional execution, *34*
Configuration files, *118*
Configuring the editor, *114*
Connecting commands with pipes, *106*
Converting a foreground process into a job, *243*
Copying and moving text, *112*
Copying files and directories, *137*
Copyleft, *8, 11*
cp, *32, 137 - 138, 140*
CPU, *238*
crc value, *230*
Creating derectories, *134*
Creating files and modifying timestamps, *145*
cron, *212, 214*
crontab, *206, 211, 215, 217*
Customizing the prompt, *95*
cut, *76, 153, 167, 174, 176, 178, 200*

D

date, *34, 206 - 207*
Deleting directories, *136*
diff, *153, 181, 190*
Digital unix, *123*
Directory, *106*
dirs, *82 - 83*
Disk access, *236*
Disk space, *236*
Displaying the command history, *67*
du, *139*
Duplicating streams, *103*

E

echo, *75 - 76*
ed, *128*
Editing a command, *60*
Editor, *71*
EGID, Effective gid, *237*
egrep, *128, 130 - 131*
emacs, *78, 108*
Entering commands, *59*
ENV, *65, 94*
Environment variables, *74*
Error stream, *99*
esps, *125*
EUID, Effective uid, *237*
ex, *113, 128*
exec, *104*
Executable file, *144, 236*
expand, *153, 201, 203*

F

fc, *67 - 68, 70 - 73*
FCEDIT, *71*
fg, *244*
file, *145*
File creation mask, *48, 137*
File type, *145*
Filename completion, *58*
Filesystem hierarchy standard, *16, 18*
Filters, *99, 152*
find, *147 - 149*
Finding files and directories, *147*
fmt, *153, 204*
fold, *153, 204*
Foreground, *243*
fsck, *19*
FSF, *8, 58*

G

Games, *118*
GID, *25 - 26, 35, 143*
GNU, *8, 197*
grep, *99, 128 - 129, 131, 153, 174, 238*
Groups, *26, 145*
gunzip, *228 - 230*
gzip, *227 - 230, 232 - 233*

H

hash, *85 - 86*
head, *152, 158*
histexpand, *78*
HISTFILE, *66*
HISTFILESIZE, *66*
history, *67*
HISTSIZE, *67*
HOME, *25, 66, 75, 82, 219, 223*

I

id, *32, 35*
ignoreeof, *78*
Immediate substitution, *72*
include, *19*
INitializing the environment, *93*
inode, *142*
Input stream, *99*
IRIX, *123*

J

Job control, *58*
Job management, *239 - 240*
Jobs, *122, 124, 241*
join, *152, 162*

K

Keyword, *87*
kill, *239, 241, 243*
KORN-SHELL, *11, 31, 58, 66, 91, 95, 98, 213, 240 - 241*

L

Lempel-Ziv alogorithm, *227 - 228*
less, *154*
lib, *20*
Library functions, *118*
Link, *144*
Linus Torvalds, *8*
login, *25, 30*
Login user name, *24*
logname, *35, 75*
lpc, *125*
lpq, *124, 214*
lpr, *99, 123*
lprm, *124, 214*
ls, *33, 76, 92, 99, 101, 102, 106, 139, 141, 183*

M

MacOs, *16*
Magic number, *230*
mail, *218, 223*
mailx, *223*
man, *20, 119*
mbox, *223*
mesg, *218, 222*
Message commands, *218*
Meta-characters, *89 - 92, 128*
mkdir, *134 - 136*
monitor, *78*
more, *152, 154 - 155, 157*
Moving around in text, *109*
Moving files and directories, *139*
MS-DOS, *16, 108, 199*
mv, *140*

N

Nedit, *70*
New filesystem layout, *16*
newgrp, *28, 41*
news, *218*
noclobber, *78, 101*
noglob, *78*
nohash, *78, 85*
notify, *78*

O

OLDPWD, *75, 81*
On-line help, *118*
Opening a new stream, *104*
Output stream, *99*
owner, *145*
owner groups, *10, 44*

P

pack, *226, 230, 233*
Parsing the command line, *92*
passwd, *38, 40, 54, 119*
Password, *24, 30, 39*
paste, *152, 163 - 164*
patch, *187 - 188, 190*
PATH, *17, 85, 87*
Permissions, *48, 50 - 52, 54, 143, 145, 222, 227, 237*
pg, *154*
Physical links, *143*
PID, *237 - 241*
Pipe, *106, 144*
Pipeline, *106, 233*
popd, *82, 84 - 85*
POSIX, *9, 129 - 130, 176, 197, 217*
POSIXLY_CORRECT, *142 - 143*
PRE, *92*
print, *149*
PRINTER, *123*
Process management, *236*
Processing file contents, *152*
procinfo, *236*
ps, *238*
PS1, *75, 95*
PS2, *75*
PS3, *75*
PS4, *75*
pushd, *82 - 84*
pwd, *80*
PWD, *75, 80 - 81*

Q

Queues, *122*

R

Ready, *236*
REAL, *237*
Real GID, RGID, *237*
Redirecting input, *102*
Redirecting output, *101*
Redirecting standard streams, *101*
Redirection, *102*
Regular expressions, *112, 128 - 129*
Relative path, *17*
Replacing characters or character strings, *111*
Requests, *122*
Resources, *236*
rev, *153, 205*
rm, *86, 140*
rmdir, *136 - 137*
root, *24, 26, 34, 45, 125, 138, 222*
RUID, Real UID, *237*

S

sbin, *20*
SCO UNIX, *244*
sed, *32, 128*
set, *60, 75, 77, 79, 101*
setuid, *237*
SGID, *54 - 55*
Shadow, *39*
Shell, *75*
Shell built-in command, *62, 75 - 76, 87, 92*
Shell-external commands, *92*
SIGCONT, *239*
SIGINT, *239, 240, 245*
SIGKILL, *239 - 240*
SIGSTOP, *239*
SIGTERM, *240*
SIGTSTP, *243, 245*
Socket, *144*
sort, *152, 165, 167, 170 - 171*
Sort key, *168 - 169*
source cmd, *71*

Special characters, *89 - 92, 128 - 129*
Special files, *118, 222*
Special operator, *128*
split, *152, 160*
Spool, *122*
Standard error, *100*
Standard input, *100, 102, 180*
Standard output, *100*
Standard streams, *100*
Sticky Bit, *54*
Stopped, *237*
Streams, *98*
Structure of a command, *98*
STTY, *244*
SUID, *54 - 55*
SunOS, *123*
System calls, *118*
System management commands, *118*
System security, *38*
System V, *11, 27, 44 - 45, 58, 122, 197, 226*

T

tail, *152, 158*
talk, *218, 225*
tcsh, *58, 66*
textedit, *70*
time, *206, 209*
Time management, *206*
Time zone, *207*
times, *206, 210*
Timestamp, *146, 219, 229 - 230*
tmp, *20*
touch, *145 - 146*
tr, *153, 178, 196*
tty, *35, 238*
type, *87 - 89*

(kernel version 2.0 à 2.2)

U

UID, *24 - 25, 35, 143, 237*
unalias, *66*
uname, *36*
uncompact, *226*
uncompress, *227, 233*
Unconditional execution, *34*
unexpand, *153, 203*
uniq, *153, 194*
umask, *49*
unpack, *226*
Users, *24, 44, 75*

V

vi, *59, 62, 70, 78, 108, 128, 155 - 156*
vi cmd, *71*
Viewing files and directories, *141*
VISUAL, *215*
vmlinuz, *141*
vmstat, *236*

W

Waiting, *237*
wall, *218, 222*
wc, *103, 152, 159 - 160*
which, *89*
who, *37, 200*
whoami, *34, 37*
Windows NT, *108*
write, *218, 220*

X

X11, *70*
xedit, *70*
xterm, *94*
xtrace, *78*

Z

zcat, *227, 230, 233*
zip, *230*
Zombie, *237*